LAUGH
AFTER
LAUGH

Other books by Raymond A. Moody, Jr., M.D.

Life after Life
Reflections on Life after Life

LAUGH
AFTER
LAUGH

The Healing Power
of Humor

Raymond A. Moody, Jr., M.D.

HEADWATERS PRESS
Jacksonville, Florida

PUBLISHED BY HEADWATERS PRESS

FOR INFORMATION WRITE P.O. BOX 41544

JACKSONVILLE, FLORIDA 32203

DISTRIBUTED BY J.B. LIPPINCOTT COMPANY

PHILADELPHIA   NEW YORK   TORONTO

**With much love
for Aye Jaye
(God bless you and everybody you hug!)
and
for our Boss,
the Man with the shovel.**

Acknowledgments

In all probability, few other physicians enjoy the privilege which I do of having, as one of my very best friends, a full-time professional clown, one who has entertained millions of children (and their parents!) There is no way fully to thank him for all that he has done to make this book possible; dedicating it to him, although still inadequate, was the best way I could think of to show my gratitude.

In addition, a veritable army of people has contributed to this venture, and I would like to express my appreciation to them for what they have done. Marilyn Mestayer and Sally Branam, my secretaries (but, more than that, my friends) through their efforts in handling my correspondence, freed me to write. Susan Corbin, even without being asked, took it upon herself to do library research. My friend, Tom Hunter, M.D., offered encouragement and shared some valuable references and insights during a serendipitous reunion on an airline flight. Reverend Bill Smith, our minister, contributed by lending some of his own reflections on the theology of laughter (and also by going to the 'rasslin' with me!) J.P. Jones (Advisor, brother-in-law, attorney, friend, manager, etc., etc.,) helped in what are quite literally too many ways to list. Rebekah Ben Verlyn gave me references, suggestions and lots of laughter. Rosalind McKnight organized the first humor workshop I led. Betty Ann Dobbins visited libraries in search of material and typed and retyped the manuscript beyond all normal limits. Matilda McQuaid aided in xeroxing and assembling the manuscripts. Peggy Williams copy edited the manuscript. John Egle, as always, is to be thanked for his sound advice and provocative questioning. C.O. Plyler, M.D., and Sister Catherine, of St. Vincent's Medical Center, Jacksonville, Florida, amazed me by assembling—almost overnight—a receptive, intelligent, and patient audience who kindly spent a weekend listening and thinking so that I would have the benefit of their response to the ideas in this book. The McDonalds Corporation permitted me to attend one of their Ronald McDonald clown seminars which gave me a unique opportunity to observe professional humorists talking shop. Ian Stevenson, M.D., brought to my attention his own findings regarding the relationship of certain pleasurable emotional states to distressing organic symptoms. Charlie Morgan selflessly gave valuable guidance concerning publication, and his wife, Marabel, helped by her enthusiastic listening. John Grove, Jr. shared his vast store of publishing and printing experience. The people at Newcomb Hall Bookstore were quick to obtain needed books for me, and John Herring took the time to listen and to give me a needed lead. Spencer Thornton, M.D., an old and a new friend, discussed this project with me, and his reception of it had much to do with my pressing onward with it.

My wife, Louise, more than deserves her own M.D., just for the medical research she has done for this book. Finally, I would like especially to thank my little boys—Avery and Palmer—because they keep me laughing!

Any mistakes and shortcomings in this volume are mine. Whatever there is of value in it flows entirely from the kindliness and love of all the wonderful and delightful people I've listed above.

Raymond A. Moody, Jr., Ph.D., M.D.
Headwaters, Virginia
July 2, 1978

Contents

"... the old man laughed loud and joyously,
shook up the details of his anatomy from head
to foot, and ended by saying that such a laugh
was money in a man's pocket, because it cut
down the doctor's bills like everything."

MARK TWAIN

in *Tom Sawyer*

Introduction

This is a book about the medical implications and uses of laughter and the sense of humor, about laughter and humor as they bear upon questions of health and disease. Now, at first thought it may seem somewhat strange that someone should think about putting these two apparently incongruous concepts—humor and medicine—together. So, perhaps I should indicate briefly how, as a physician, my attention was drawn to this subject.

First of all, I have always been a repressed humorist, and as a child one of the very first things I ever wanted to become when I grew up was a professional comedian. Humor has always played a big part in my life and in my response to people and situations. I am an inveterate practical joker and punster, and I love to laugh. Naturally, I carried these tendencies along with me into medical school when I entered training.

Second, over the years I have encountered a surprising number of instances in which, to all appearances, patients have laughed themselves back to health, or at least have used their sense of humor as a very positive and adaptive response to their illnesses. These remarkable recoveries, some of which are detailed in the next chapter, have suggested to me the possibility that there may indeed be something therapeutic about humor, just as folk belief has long assured us.

Third, a significant insight gradually dawned on me as I continued my studies in medical school. I was told during my training that I should try to find out about each patient's appetite, sexual functioning, habits of sleep, nutrition and elimination. I was carefully instructed to take note of any peculiarities of language, appearance, complexion, posture, and gait. Great emphasis was placed on how essential it was to record carefully on hospital charts and various other forms, the patient's age, occupation, marital status, general level of intelligence, weight, blood pressure, heart rate, respiration rate, and a host of other parameters, evaluating each as to whether it was normal or abnormal. In fact, at one time or other I was explicitly directed to take note of almost every kind of information about my patients that one can imagine. However, not once in all those years of training do I remember anyone reminding me to probe into their sense of humor or to observe and to record how willing they were to smile or laugh. Yet, as time has gone on, I have come to feel that a human being's ability to laugh and to appreciate funny material is just as important a fact about him, and just as valuable and valid an indicator of the state of his health, as are all those other things.

Furthermore, as I began to learn by experience how valuable an aid humor is in assessing the state of someone's physical and emotional health, it became apparent—little by little—that humor and health are not unrelated notions at all. As will be amply demonstrated later on, the connection between laughter and health is drawn almost universally, by laymen and medical professionals alike, in ancient writings as well as in the most up-to-date medical journals. Indeed, in all probability one reason why the relationship was never explicitly pointed out to me in medical school or in subsequent training is simply that it is so obvious. The ability to laugh is one of the most characteristic and deep-seated features of man. Many psychologists and philosophers have even argued that man is the only creature who laughs or has a sense of humor; some have taken this so far as to suggest that man might be defined as "the risible animal," the animal who can laugh. Accordingly, a person's sense of humor is such an important aspect of him that it is something which others notice almost automatically, without thinking much about it. It is only in cases in which there is something extreme or inappropriate about someone's laughter or sense of humor that it is likely to enter another's conscious awareness. Otherwise, it probably wouldn't seem worthy of notice at all.

No doubt, then, doctors have probably always noted— even if only preconsciously—their patients' senses of humor. Nonetheless, probably in part because of its obvious and almost unconsciously appreciated significance, the role of humor in health is one which hardly ever is openly and explicitly discussed. To my knowledge, no medical schools offer courses or lecture series on the topic, and—even in our paper-oriented society—there is probably not a single health form on which there is a space for checking off whether or not the patient's sense of humor seems normal.

The automatic, unconscious nature of our recognition of another person's sense of humor, however, may be only part of the explanation for the dearth of open discussion of the subject. Is it possible that another factor lies in what the psychologist Gordon Allport has called the "tenderness taboo"? He has pointed out that academicians seem as a group to be more comfortable investigating negative mental states and emotions—hostility, aggression, anger, greed, depression, anxiety—than they are studying positive ones— love, elation, altruism, sympathy, generosity, understanding, humor. At times, indeed, it appears that as an institution professional psychology is somewhat embarrassed to dwell upon these more happy states.

There are reasons in the present instance, though, for going on and breaking the taboo, and for articulating the obvious. In the first place, as a society we appear to have become obsessed with the notion that there ought to be a pill or an operation or a machine to treat each illness. We tend to think that the doctor should be able to cure us—instantaneously, preferably—of any ailment, with a minimum of effort or cooperation on our own part. Such magical attitudes about the efficacy of modern technological medicine have led to a neglect of the very real factors of emotion and mental outlook which may precipitate disease, and affect its course, duration, and outcome. Hopefully, focusing for a while on the relationship between humor and health may help to correct this imbalance, at least to some degree.

Also, if it is important to notice someone's sense of humor when assessing his health, then it helps for the clinician to have in mind some sort of systematic classification of the conditions in which changes or malfunctions in laughter or humor indicate the presence of disease. This requires a more highly reflective and well-articulated approach to the subject than has heretofore been taken.

In addition, the instances of apparent healing by humor are somewhat puzzling in that, taken by themselves, they seem difficult to explain. In fact, a natural response for a person trained in modern medicine to make to these reports would be: "But this is just anecdotal. There are no experimental controls," or "But these people probably would have gotten better anyway!" Such objections are valid and are to be taken seriously.

My only point, for the present, is that observations of this type, coupled with the longstanding folk belief in the value of laughter as a remedy, at least suggest that there may be something here which is worth looking into. We will see that while almost everyone pays lip service to the proverbial curative value of humor and laughter almost no one has taken the time to investigate it. Accordingly, it may be that bringing into public discussion some ideas along these lines will encourage researchers to follow up with specific studies.

So, for these reasons and for others that will become apparent later on, I have written a book on the medical aspects of laughter. It is not a book of pat answers; it is a book of observations and an assertion that perhaps we need to look into some unusual facts which we have not so far tried to explain. Indeed, some of them seem rather difficult to explain from the point of view of our current understanding of the human mind and body. I should hope that what follows will be taken as a source of challenging puzzles. For doctors, I hope that it will help stimulate us to come up with some new ways of capturing some of the energy people use in laughing and to put it to work in helping them to get better, in short, to harness the healing power of humor for our patients.

I

A Doctor Looks at Laughter

Before we can proceed properly with this exploration, our first task is to define, or at least more clearly to characterize, laughter and the sense of humor. We need to take note of some rather striking facts about laughter and humor, so that some of the points and observations to be made and discussed later on will be more understandable.

The initial question one would need to ask about anything one is discussing is: "What *is* it?" This question is deceptively simple in the case of laughter. Because we are so accustomed to experiencing it as an automatic, spontaneous response, we are seldom consciously aware of what a complex activity it is physiologically. Yet, we immediately become aware of this complexity as soon as we are asked to formulate a verbal description of laughing. To bring home that point, one need only quote the following description, drawn from an article published in a scientific journal around the turn of the century.

There occur in laughter and more or less in smiling, clonic spasms of the diaphragm in number ordinarily about eighteen perhaps, and contraction of most of the muscles of the face. The upper side of the mouth and its corners are drawn upward. The upper eyelid is elevated, as are also, to some extent, the brows, the skin over the glabella, and the upper lip, while the skin at the outer canthi of the eyes is characteristically puckered. The nostrils are moderately dilated and drawn upward, the tongue slightly extended, and the cheeks distended and drawn somewhat upward; in persons with the pinnal muscles largely developed, the pinnae tend to incline forwards. The lower jaw vibrates or is somewhat withdrawn (doubtless to afford all possible air to the distending lungs), and the head, in extreme laughter, is thrown backward; the trunk is straightened even to the beginning of bending backward, until (and this usually happens soon), fatigue-pain in the diaphragm and accessory abdominal muscles causes a marked proper flexion of the trunk for its relief. The whole arterial vascular system is dilated, with consequent blushing from the effect on the dermal capillaries of the face and neck, and at times of the scalp and hands. From this same cause in the main the eyes often slightly bulge forwards and the lachrymal gland becomes active, ordinarily to a degree only to cause a "brightening" of the eyes, but often to such an extent that the tears overflow entirely their proper channels.[1]

Although that description has proper Victorian thoroughness, some might prefer Sir Francis Bacon's more succinct, but somehow more colorful and lively one:

. . . laughter causeth a dilation of the mouth and lips; a continued expulsion of the breath, with a loud noise, which maketh the interjection of laughing, shaking of the breasts and sides; running of the eyes with water, if it be violent and continued.[2]

2

Defining "the sense of humor" is much more difficult, however. This phrase has a number of different, though interrelated, meanings which seem to me to lie along a spectrum with more egocentric interpretations of the concept at one end, and more universal understandings at the opposite end. Let me illustrate this by describing six different kinds of things one might be implying about someone simply by saying that he has a "good sense of humor," beginning with the "most egocentric" meaning and going through the "most universalistic" meaning of the phrase.

(1) *The "He-Realizes-How-Funny-I-Am" Sense.* I may mean, by saying that another person has a good sense of humor, little or nothing more than that I can easily get him to laugh whenever I want him to. Although this may be quite flattering to my ego, it is of rather minimal interest in considering the medical aspects of humor and laughter.

(2) *The Conventional Sense.* By imputing a good sense of humor to someone else, I may mean that he laughs, not necessarily *at* me, but, rather, at the same *kinds* of things (jokes, movies, cartoons, etc.) that I appreciate as being funny. Or, more universally still, I may mean that he laughs, fairly easily, at the same kinds of things that other people who are members of his sub-culture, society, or culture find amusing and laughable. As will become apparent later, this sense has a bit more relevance for the topic of medicine and humor, especially when one is considering the use of aberrations of laughter and humor in diagnosing illnesses of one kind or another.

(3) *The "Life-of-the-Party" Sense.* I may also mean, by saying that a person has a good sense of humor, that that person has an excellent repertoire of good jokes, that he has

3

memorized a large number of funny stories, and that he is skilled at repeating them for the amusement of others. In this sense, I mean that he is able to make others, including me, laugh at his stories and/or antics.

(4) *The Creative Sense.* A person who has "a good sense of humor" in the creative sense is one whose creativity manifests itself in the production of new, original humorous remarks, stories, jokes, plays, etc. Professional writers of jokes and other humorous material display this talent to a more conspicuous degree than most of their fellow human beings, but people with such talent are obviously found in all walks of life.

(5) *The "Good Sport" Sense.* In this sense of the phrase, a person with a good sense of humor is one who can, we say, "take a joke," or "laugh at himself," or "enjoy a joke at his own expense." In a way, what one is saying when one makes such a remark about another person is more a statement about something he *doesn't* do; namely, he doesn't blow up into a rage, pout and fume, or become overtly defensive or hostile when someone else "kids" him. Later, it will become apparent that this sense, too, assumes some diagnostic significance in psychiatry.

(6) *The "Cosmic Perspective" Sense.* Finally, there is another, still broader meaning of the phrase, and one which I think is ultimately the most relevant when we come to consider the explanation of whatever "health-giving" value there might be in mirth. In this sense, a person with "a good sense of humor" is one who can see himself and others in the world in a somewhat distant and detached way. He views life from an altered perspective in which he can laugh at, yet remain in contact with and emotionally involved with people and events in a positive way. Such a person has the ability to

4

perceive life comically without thereby losing any love or respect for himself or for humanity in general.

Laughter and humor are phenomena which, in order to be understood, must be looked at and evaluated from numerous, interrelated perspectives. It will be convenient, for our present purposes, to examine some facts and observations about humor and laughter in terms of physiological, psychological, and social aspects.

PHYSIOLOGICAL ASPECTS

Laughter and Muscle Tone. It is well-documented by laboratory experiment,[3] and fairly apparent from common observation as well, that laughter is accompanied by a decrease in tone of the skeletal muscles of the body. Sometimes, we just seem to become weak all over, occasionally even to the point of collapsing, when we are seized by a fit of good, hearty laughter. Many have observed, no doubt, that they may have difficulty grasping an object tightly while laughing vigorously. This fact may have something to do with why we characterize laughing as "breaking up." The feeling we sometimes experience, while laughing, that the muscles have suddenly gone limp, may also partly explain why numerous theorists, over the years, have pointed out that laughter involves a release of tension or a release of surplus energy. For instance, the nineteenth century British philosopher Herbert Spencer[4] characterized laughter as a "discharge of excess nervous excitement," and Sigmund Freud[5] made a similar conception the cornerstone of his theory of laughter.

"Reflex" Laughter on Being Tickled. A reflex is an auto-

5

matic, involuntary response to a stimulus. It occurs as a function, not of conscious thought or will, but rather of the ways in which the cells of the nervous system are structurally arranged and of how they function. The knee-jerk response is the classical example: A tap at a certain spot on someone's knee sends his leg swinging upward. The study of reflex reactions of this kind falls squarely within the province of physiology.

Laughter may occur from other causes than the observance of humorous material, and being tickled is prominent among them. A person who is being tickled automatically makes movements which resemble those he might make were he defending himself against an attack. He resists and struggles, trying to push the other person's hands away, and the part of his body which is being tickled withdraws with a jerk. In addition, he often laughs uproariously, uncontrollably. Since, at least superficially, the conscious and cognitive element so apparent in the response to jokes is apparently absent, some have classified the laughter which occurs as a reaction to tickling as a reflex.

Laughter and Other Diaphragmatic Phenomena. The diaphragm—the large muscle of inspiration which separates the chest cavity from the abdominal cavity—is actively involved in laughter. It is of some importance to note that laughter is sometimes related in an interesting way to other phenomena involving the diaphragm. Hearty laughter is frequently followed, in some individuals, by episodes of hiccoughing or coughing. For instance, after an all-out laughing fit, both of my children will commonly come down with the hiccoughs.

Laughter as a Convulsive Process. Mankind has always been awed by the disorder called epilepsy, so much so that at

6

certain times in history it has been thought to be a sacred disease: Its victims have been considered visionaries possessed by divine spirits, or else able to receive knowledge through channels not open to ordinary mortals. Even today, when we have learned that epileptic symptoms stem from errant electrical discharges having their focus in areas of abnormally irritable tissue in the brain, the events of an epileptic seizure remain quite dramatic, frightening, and awe-inspiring. During a *grand mal* seizure, the victim may suddenly cry out in an unintelligible manner, fall to the floor, lose control of bowel or bladder functions, foam at the mouth, and twitch uncontrollably.

Laughter, at the very least, resembles a convulsive phenomenon. We are all familiar with the phrases "convulsed with laughter" and "a fit of laughter" and find them quite natural ones to use. Indeed, many people seem to double up and to shake in an uncontrollable fashion, or even to collapse to the floor when seized with an attack of robust, hearty laughter. This behavior may even be accepted or expected as the norm. An anthropologist who studied them was greatly impressed by the way the Pygmies, when overcome with hilarity, fall to the ground. Such behavior resembles—perhaps in a not so superficial way—the movements of people undergoing epileptic seizures.

Humor Appreciation and Physiological Arousal. In one well-known study,[6] humor appreciation and physiological arousal were found to be interrelated in a most fascinating way. A group of experimental subjects was divided into three sub-groups. One sub-group was given an injection of the hormone epinephrin (adrenalin), the second sub-group an injection of plain saline (water with a small concentration of salt), and

7

the third sub-group an injection of a drug called chlorpromazine (a major tranquilizer). None of the subjects, of
course, was informed of which substance he received, or
whether it was any different from what any other subject was
given. Now, epinephrin acts upon the body as a stimulant,
and would have increased the general level of arousal of the
subjects to whom it was given. Saline is neutral in this respect,
and should have neither increased or decreased the level of
arousal. Finally, chlorpromazine as a tranquilizer, would have
tended to decrease the level of arousal of those subjects who
received it. All of the subjects were shown a movie and
subsequently were asked to rate the film with respect to how
funny it was. The result was that those who received the
epinephrin rated the movie as most humorous, those who
were injected with saline gave it intermediate funniness
ratings, and those who were given chlorpromazine failed as
a group to appreciate the humor in the film. The most
intriguing implication of these findings is that even humor,
something we generally regard as being so clearly psychological and emotional in basis, has a profound connection with
physiological states of the body.

PSYCHOLOGICAL ASPECTS

Humor, Laughter and Regression. "Regression" is a concept
which is very widely employed in psychology and psychiatry.
In essence, it is a mental mechanism whereby a person reverts
to an earlier level of mental or emotional functioning, usually
in a conscious or unconscious attempt to escape or to alleviate
a painful or overwhelming reality with which he cannot
otherwise cope. Severe regression is a prominent feature of

certain types of mental illness, such as schizophrenia. However, to a milder degree, it occurs in almost all illnesses. Most of us, when we are ill, adopt some of the behavior which we outgrew as we developed from infancy through childhood and adolescence to adulthood. When we are sick, and unable to carry out some of the tasks we have learned to do for ourselves, it is quite normal and natural to regress; our behavior says to others, "Take care of me."

In ways that will be further elaborated as we go along, humor involves regression. For example, jokes may involve childish misuses of language. Some authorities have compared the antics of clowns to the childish, regressed behavior of some psychotically disturbed persons.

Perhaps regression of a mild type is also the basis of an odd occurrence I have noticed on numerous occasions—as I am sure many others have—and have often wondered how to explain. Sometimes a group of people who are staying up late, past their customary bedtimes, become exceedingly "giggly." Remarks or incidents that wouldn't have seemed amusing at 4:00 p.m. become hilariously funny at 1:00 a.m., and everyone is laughing and giggling at these silly things. There is a partial regression to earlier developmental levels which accompanies the gradual onset of sleep. As one drifts by degrees more deeply into sleep, things which would not seem reasonable or logical if the mind were fully alert may suddenly seem to "make sense." This regression of the reasoning faculties is accompanied by regression in other behavior as well. For instance, as the person lies down, he may even curl up into the fetal position.

Although this is speculative, it is interesting to conjecture that this "late night hilarity" is another manifestation of

9

the regression associated with encroaching sleep. That is, the mind, not fully alert, may slip back to earlier, more primitive and childish modes of humor appreciation. Of course, one must not ignore alternative, physiological interpretations of the same behavior. Perhaps, as in yawning, it is merely that the body is making an attempt, by allowing more laughter, to bring in more oxygen.

Laughter as an Expressive Occurrence. One has a sense, in thinking about laughter, that it has an almost *explosive* character, that through it feelings and emotions erupt from the inside of us into the outside world. One of the best ways of appreciating this is by remembering how necessary it is, at certain times, to keep one's amusement to oneself. For there may be times when the social occasion is not appropriate for its expression. For example, to laugh may be unkind, or might reveal the presence of the laughing person, or might even provoke others to punish him. In situations like these, the expressive force of laughter becomes very obvious (perhaps even uncomfortable) through the counter force needed to stifle it.

Different individuals adopt different methods of doing this. Many people say that they bite their lips or the insides of their cheeks to hold in the laughter. A psychiatrist friend of mine told me that if he gets into this predicament he finds himself shaking his crossed leg very vigorously in order to discharge the excess energy he finds welling up inside of him and demanding release. The associates of the mad Emperor Commodus of Rome were sometimes so amused by his insane antics that they almost burst into laughter. To do so in his presence, however, might well have resulted in their summary execution. So, they contrived the practice of chewing the leaves from their garlands of laurel, in order to force back their incipient mirth.

All in all, this expressive-explosive feature of laughter is an interesting one. It may have something to do, I suppose, with a question which, to my knowledge, has never been extensively investigated: Why is it that when some people try to tell a lie, or are caught in a fib, they begin to smile, or even erupt into laughter?

The Relationship between Laughing and Weeping. We customarily think of laughing and weeping as opposites, an attitude which is expressed by the adoption of the laughing and frowning masks as the symbols of, respectively, comedy and tragedy in the theater. In actual fact, however, the relationship between them is not nearly so simple. Laughter may be accompanied or followed by weeping, and it is the flow of tears which gives the bright, twinkling appearance to the eyes which is so characteristic of the hearty laugh.

Some emotions may call forth laughter, tears, or both. I remember a recent occasion when this was brought home to me in a dramatic way. I have made several appearances in recent years as a semi-professional comedian. I was surprised at one of these shows when I saw two women on the front row who were to all appearances crying. Tears were streaming down their faces, and they were wiping them away with their handkerchiefs. Since the rest of the audience seemed amused, I was momentarily taken aback, until I realized that their tears were from mirth, and not from distress.

Laughter as the Opposite of Certain Negative Emotions. Although it is difficult to state with any great precision, there does seem to be some sense in which humor, laughter, and mirth are, in effect, the opposite of certain negative emotional states, such as anger, or a vengeful or punishing attitude. It may even be that a humorous attitude toward certain situations precludes, or is inconsistent with, the adoption of a straightforwardly vengeful attitude toward those situations. Thus, if parents were to reflect upon it, they would no doubt agree that they find it difficult or impossible to punish their children if they first succumb to laughter about what the youngsters have done. Creatively humorous individuals frequently put this psychological principle to practical use in avoiding potentially violent encounters. Many examples of this could be cited. The following one, drawn from a book about Richard Tarlton, the reknowned funnyman who served Queen Elizabeth I, illustrates it nicely even though it contains prejudicial overtones we find reprehensible today.

As Tarlton and others passed along Fleet Street, he espied a spruce young gallant, black of complexion, with long haire hanging downe over his eares, and his beard of the Italian cut, in white sattin very quaintly cut, and his body so stiffely starcht, that he could not bend himselfe any way for no gold. Tarlton seing such a wonder comming, trips before him, and, meeting this gallant, tooke the wall of him, knowing that one so proud at least looked for the prerogative. The gallant, scorning that a player should take the wall, or so much indignifie[2] him, turnes himselfe, and presently drew his rapier. Tarlton drew likewise. The gentleman fell to it roundly; but Tarlton, in his owne defence, compassing and taversing his ground,[3] gaped with a wide mouth, whereat the people laughed. The gentleman, pausing, enquired why he gaped so. O, ar, saies he, in hope to swallow you; for, by my troth, you seeme to me like a prune in a messe of white broth. At this the people

12

parted them. The gentleman noting his mad humour, went his way well contented; for he knew not how to amend it.[7]

SOCIAL ASPECTS

The Contagiousness of Laughter. As every comedian and every elementary school teacher knows, laughter is socially contagious. In a grammar school classroom, if one or two children start giggling, soon all of the pupils will be doing the same. There are few ways of stopping a mini-epidemic of this type; it must wind down and stop of its own accord. Another excellent way of observing the infectious quality of laughter is by playing a party game called "belly laugh." Participants form a human chain, with the head of each person lying on the abdomen of someone else. Soon someone starts laughing, and the laughter proceeds in a contagious wave right around the room; shortly everyone is laughing.

In passing, it is interesting to ponder why some other apparently automatic responses of the diaphragm or respiratory apparatus share this contagious quality of laughter, while others do not. Hiccoughing, for example, does not seem to be contagious under normal circumstances. However, as actors who appear in stage productions can testify, coughing is contagious; only one member of a large audience need cough and soon a chorus of hacking is reverberating through the theater. Similarly, if one person in a group yawns, several others will soon follow. One way I have always used to help my children drift off to sleep at night is to rock them for a while and then to yawn loudly. Within moments, they are yawning, too; soon they are drowsy, and I can tuck them into bed with no protests.

13

The Social Power of Laughter. Laughter, mobilized in the form of ridicule and satire, has always been a potent social force. At one time, duels of ridicule were established practice among the Eskimos of Greenland. Instead of resorting to physical violence or bloodshed to settle their grievances against one another, the angered parties would instead publicly deride and insult one another. These contests took place in public and, before the eyes of their assembled tribal community, the participants mocked, abused, and made fun of one another, to the accompaniment of drums, often reciting traditional ludicrous songs passed on in the tribe for just this purpose. The spectators were greatly amused, and expressed their appreciation by jolly laughter. The bouts were taken quite seriously; losers were sometimes so humiliated that they went into exile. Among the Japanese, one of the primary ways of disciplining children is apparently to warn them that if they behave in certain ways, other people will laugh at them. Among many other groups, including the Pygmies, being laughed at is one of the most dreaded and feared kinds of punishments or social sanctions.

Humor and Communication. One very important social function of humor is often forgotten: Humor is a mode of communication, and has been called a "social lubricant." One excellent way we have of establishing communication with a stranger, or of re-establishing it with a friend or loved one, is to "break the ice" with a humorous remark. This way of using mirth socially has been very nicely described by the Victorian novelist George Meredith in his writings on comedy.

> Each one of an affectionate couple may be willing, as we say, to die for the other, yet unwilling to utter the

14

agreeable word at the right moment; but if the wits were
sufficiently quick for them to perceive that they are in a
comic situation, as affectionate couples must be when
they quarrel, they would not wait for the moon or the
almanac . . . to bring back the flood-tide of tender
feelings, that they should join hands and lips.[8]

Humor as Work. Comedy is organized within our society
as an occupation. The subculture constituted by comic actors, comedians, and writers who create humorous material
has not been studied in any depth by social scientists, and so
is a fertile field for investigation. Entrance into the profession,
although it can occur rather spontaneously, seems to be at
least partly governed by informal and unwritten rules, pred-
icated on the individual's recognition or sponsorship by
influential comic entertainers. Comedians share a common
terminology of "shop talk." Clubs of comedians exist in
several large cities. It is hard to estimate the ultimate influence of these professionals in shaping public opinion, since
humor is so ubiquitous, but it must be significant, for there is
a great demand for amusing entertainment. The so-called
situation comedies are perennially the most popular shows
on television in the United States.

This catalog of some assorted physiological, psychological, and social aspects of humor and laughter is a convenient
but also a highly artificial way of presenting these facts about
mirth. For, these three dimensions of laughter and humor are
not at all clearly separable. Rather they are interwoven and
interrelated in a complicated and bewildering way. To
choose only one example, in the scheme above, the laughter
which results from being tickled was labeled a "reflex" and
therefore classified as a physiological matter. It is not to be

imagined that things are that simple in reality, however. For there are psychological and social implications of tickling as well. Studies have shown that infants are far more likely to respond with laughter when they are tickled by a familiar, loving figure (their mother or father) than they are if they are tickled by someone whom they don't know. Indeed, if a stranger tickles a baby, the child is likely to respond by crying. From the broad perspective of human experience one should remember that, at various times, tickling has been used as a method of torture. The Romans, among others, employed it as a cruel punishment.

Let us bring this section to a close with a final note: Laughter has intrigued mankind throughout history and has spawned hundreds of treatises and tomes. Most of these volumes seem to have been addressed to the question: "What makes people laugh?" This venerable controversy has thus far been relatively fruitless, and new theories continue to be spawned and debated, accepted as obvious by some and derided as mistaken and groundless by others. In what follows, I shall attempt to steer clear of this controversy. Instead, what I want to consider is a question of much greater practical import. For, throughout the centuries of academic debate about the causes and occasions of laughter, the still, small voice of folk wisdom and of common sense has been whispering to us, "Laughter is good for you!" The task of this book is simply to ask whether and to what extent this may be so.

II

Healing by Humor: Some Examples

At one time during my medical training I was treating a middle-aged man who was suffering from chronic depression. He had almost constant headaches and complained, as depressed persons so often do, of insomnia—of awakening in the early morning hours and being unable to get back to sleep. He was chronically unable to say no to other people who made unreasonable demands on him. This man had essentially no formal education and for that reason was unable to get a satisfactory job. At that time he was working in an intolerable setting, in a cookie factory.

As I talked with this fellow during our first few psychotherapeutic sessions, he consistently maintained a gloomy countenance. For week after week he kept coming to me, never once smiling, with tale after tale of his troubles, while I tried unsuccessfully to steer him into the public education which was available to him at no cost. I felt that there was a strong situational component to his depression, and that further training would give him more self-confidence and enable him to get a better job, thus, improving his life situation. However, he had been steadfastly resisting my efforts.

One day when he came in for his appointment, he related in a most woebegone fashion, that a new foreman had come to work in the factory. The new boss had sized up the situation, had expressed dissatisfaction with the rate of cookie production, and had talked of an increase. My patient had weakly protested that the wrapping machine just would not function any more quickly, but to no avail. The decision was made, the order was given, and the cookie production was speeded up. True to my patient's prediction, the wrapping machine went haywire, and soon an avalanche of cookies was spewing all over everything. Helpless before the onslaught of cookies, my patient had stood there while the boss railed at him, the only person who had challenged the scheme in the first place.

Sitting there as he related the story to me, I conjured up an image of it in my mind. As I contemplated the scene, try as I did to prevent myself, I did something which I had been constantly told that I should never do. Despite the fact that I was biting the inside of my cheeks to try to prevent it, I felt the corners of my mouth begin to form into a smile. Amazingly, my patient, responding, began to smile, and then he burst out into peals of laughter.

It is interesting that this event started the therapeutic relationship between us anew. From that point on, I believe that he got better. I think that in that moment, standing back from his life situation and seeing it from a comic—even perhaps cosmic—perspective, he realized that he had been playing a game with himself. It really was up to him to get himself out of his troubling life situation. Subsequently, he resolved to do something about it. He went into a training program so that he could obtain more gratifying employment.

There are reports, both in the professional literature and in the context of anecdote and folk belief, of persons who have been cured, or at least eased, in numerous medical and/or psychological conditions, by the use of laughter and humor.

One of the most remarkable of these is an account published in the conservative *New England Journal of Medicine*, one of the most respected medical journals in the world. In it, Mr. Norman Cousins, at the time editor of *The Saturday Review*,[1] detailed his remarkable recovery from a grave and potentially life-threatening illness. Following a stressful incident at the end of an emotionally and physically draining trip abroad, Mr. Cousins noted the onset of a fever and feelings of achiness and malaise during his flight home to the United States. His illness progressed and soon after his return he was admitted to the hospital, where clinical and laboratory findings indicated that he was suffering from a serious collagen disease. Collagen is a substance found in the connective tissue of the body which is essential in holding the cells and larger structures of the body together. In Mr. Cousins' case, involvement was so extreme that he soon experienced great difficulty and pain in moving his joints, and he was told that his prospects for recovery were in no way favorable.

He refused to accept his grim prognosis, and—with the sympathetic understanding of his physician—he decided to take charge of his own treatment. He remembered reading of the role of the endocrine system in fighting disease, and of the adverse consequences of negative emotional states on the chemical balance of the body. He reasoned that, if negative emotions played any part in predisposing him to the illness, then perhaps positive emotions could restore the balance and aid in his recovery.

He already was gifted with a vigorous will to live, and he resolved to help it along by the use of mirth. He obtained some funny movies—specifically, some old *Candid Camera* segments—and had them shown to him by his nurse. He noted that laughter was a powerful analgesic; one ten-minute interlude of laughter would yield two hours of painless sleep. In addition, and even more remarkably, it was found that an important medical test for inflammation, made before and after each session of laughter, showed cumulative improvement.

Mr. Cousins' self-prescribed regimen included other components as well. Disgruntled with the non-nutritious hospital food and with what he perceived as an unwarranted and too-frequent invasion of his veins for blood samples, he had checked himself out of the hospital and into the more cheerful (and less expensive) environment of a hotel. Here, he continued his humor therapy, relieved of the concern that his laughing would disturb fellow patients. He continued to improve, and at the time he wrote his account, over a decade later, was still at a vigorous level of functioning, despite realistic and informed medical predictions to the contrary.

One could always offer the objection that Mr. Cousins would have recovered anyway, even without the laughter. Or one could say, with some justice, that the results were not scientifically significant, since they represent observations of a single case. Still, it is clear that that Mr. Cousins himself believes that laughter played an important part in his recovery. Personally, on grounds other than scientific ones, I haven't any qualms about concurring with him.

One of the most fascinating uses of humor in healing has never to my knowledge been recorded in medical literature.

In fact, had I not seen it with my own eyes and gathered many reports of it, I would be rather hesitant to mention it myself. It is that sometimes, through their antics, clowns can bring people back from severely withdrawn and unresponsive states even after all attempts by their doctors and nurses have failed. It is not at all unusual for clowns to be fully aware of this; everyone I know who has been a clown for a respectable period, and who makes it his practice to visit hospitals while dressed up and "in face" has his own stories of this to tell. Doctors, as a group, are not cognizant of it.

One clown whose face is known to most American children related to me how, as he was walking through a large hospital he saw a little girl with a doll of his likeness lying beside her in bed as she was being fed by a nurse. As the clown walked in, the child said his name, whereupon the nurse threw down the spoon and dashed off to call the physician. For the child—diagnosed, he said, as catatonic—had been unresponsive for six months. The doctor was able to get her to follow up this first communication with other responses, and the child progressively improved following this break-through.

In another case, a 95-year-old man was admitted to the hospital with severe depression. He had not eaten for several days and for the same period had not said a word to anyone. His physicians were alarmed; they were concerned that he would soon die. A clown entered his hospital room and within thirty minutes had succeeded in getting the elderly man to talk, to laugh, and to eat. The man lived for several more years and the clown maintained communication with him during this time.

I have looked on as an internationally famous clown

strolled the floors of pediatric wards in hospitals. In one room we found a three-year-old boy who was so frightened and distressed at being in the hospital that he hadn't talked to anyone—the doctors, the nurses, or even his mother or father—for three weeks. He immediately responded verbally to the clown's laughable overtures, and told us goodbye as we left. Afterwards, this child, too, continued to communicate.

Apparently, this phenomenon is nothing new, for I have found a similar account in a book which dates back well over a century. Joseph Grimaldi, born in 1779, was one of the most beloved humorous entertainers the world has ever known. He appeared as a clown character known as "Joey," and through his performances exerted a formative influence on the development of the clown role as it is known all over the world today. According to his contemporaries, he was an unbelievably funny man. In his memoirs, as edited by Charles Dickens, he tells the following story:

> "In the July of this year a very extraordinary circumstance occurred at Sadler's Wells, which was the great topic of conversation in the neighborhood for some time afterwards. It happened thus:
>
> Captain George Harris, of the Royal Navy . . . had recently returned to England after a long voyage. The crew being paid off, many of the men followed their commander to London, and proceeded to enjoy themselves after the usual fashion of sailors. Sadler's Wells was at that time a famous place of resort with the blue-jackets, the gallery being sometimes almost solely occupied by seamen and their female companions. A large body of Captain Harris's men resorted hither one night, and amongst them a man who was deaf and dumb, and had been so for many years. This man was

placed by his shipmates in the front row of the gallery. Grimaldi was in great force that night, and, although the audience were in one roar of laughter, nobody appeared to enjoy his fun and humour more than this poor fellow. His companions good-naturedly took a great deal of notice of him, and one of them, who talked very well with his fingers, inquired how he liked the entertainments; to which the deaf and dumb man replied through the same medium, and with various gestures of great delight, that he had never seen anything half so comical before.

As the scene progressed Grimaldi's tricks and jokes became still more irresistible; and at length, after a violent peal of laughter and applause which quite shook the theatre and in which the dumb man joined most heartily, he suddenly turned to his mate, who sat next to him, and cried out with much glee, "What a damned funny fellow!"

"Why, Jack," shouted the other man, starting back with great surprise, "can you speak?"

"Speak!" replied the other. "Ay, that I can, and hear, too."

Upon this the whole party, of course, gave three vehement cheers, and at the conclusion of the piece adjourned in a great procession with the recovered man, elevated on the shoulders of a half dozen friends, in the centre. A crowd of people quickly assembled round the door, and great excitement and curiosity were occasioned as the intelligence ran from mouth to mouth that a deaf and dumb man had come to speak and hear, all owing to the cleverness of Joey Grimaldi.

The landlady of the tavern, thinking Grimaldi would like to see his patient, told the man that if he would call next morning he should see the actor who

23

had made him laugh so much. Grimaldi, being apprised of the circumstances, repaired to the house at the appointed time, and saw him, accompanied by several of his companions, all of whom still continued to manifest the liveliest interest in the sudden change that had happened to their friend, and kept on cheering, and drinking, and treating everybody in the house, in proof of their gratification. The man, who appeared an intelligent well-behaved fellow, said that in the early part of his life he could both speak and hear very well; and that he had attributed his deprivation of the two senses to the intense heat of the sun in the quarter of the world to which he had been, and from which he had very recently returned. He added that on the previous evening he had for a long time felt a powerful anxiety to express his delight at what was passing on the stage; and that after some feat of Grimaldi's which struck him as being particularly amusing he had made a strong effort to deliver his thoughts, in which, to his own great astonishment, no less than that of his companions, he succeeded. Mr. Charles Dibdin, who was present, put several questions to the man; and from his answers it appeared to every one present that he was speaking the truth. Indeed, his story was in some measure confirmed by Captain Harris himself; for one evening, about six months afterwards, as Grimaldi was narrating the circumstances in the green-room at Covent Garden, that gentleman, who chanced to be present, immediately remarked that he had no reason from the man's behaviour while with him to suppose him an imposter, and that he had seen him on that day in full possession of his senses.[2]

So, clowns can sometimes draw out ill persons who have

been unresponsive. This is, I believe, an important fact, for many reasons, not the least of which is that unresponsiveness greatly complicates medical treatment. If a patient will not or cannot communicate, it is much more difficult, and sometimes impossible, for his physician to tell what is wrong with him or to treat him.

More research into this is called for. We need to know what kinds of withdrawn states under what general conditions, can be improved or corrected by the ministrations of clowns. The unresponsiveness in two of the examples given above apparently stemmed from depression, and in another was a manifestation of catatonia. The Grimaldi case is ambiguous, but the sailor may have been suffering from hysteria. All these conditions will be explained more fully later, in our section on mirth in mental illnesses, but for now it can be said that they represent a wide variety of psychological problems.

Some doctors will react with a good, healthy scepticism to my claim that clowns may occasionally bring a patient out of a prolonged state of withdrawal. All I would suggest is that any doubting physician invite an experienced professional clown to visit the wards, follow along, watch, and then decide.

There are certain medical conditions in which humor, though not specifically curative, is widely recognized as an important, healthy, and desirable response. This is strikingly evident in the case of several kinds of stigmatizing medical conditions, among them, severe facial deformities.

One of the very worst psychological catastrophes that can befall a human being is to receive a disfiguring injury to the face. I am impressed that all of those patients I have seen who have adapted most successfully to such injuries seem to

25

have a good sense of humor. They have fallen back on humor in two ways. First, they have used it to help them develop an outlook from which their horrendous misfortune seems more bearable. Secondly, they employ humor successfully to solve a complicated problem in interpersonal communication which is inherent in their situation. We all depend heavily upon facial expression in regulating our communications with others, in figuring out how they feel and what they are thinking about. If someone's face is distorted and frozen by an injury, other people have a hard time comfortably talking with him.

Obviously, then, the stigmatized patients are faced with the problem of learning to put others at ease in social situations. The patients I am talking about—those who adapt favorably—solve this dilemma in communications by coming up with a repertoire of one-liners to introduce themselves. They have discovered that they can defuse the mounting tension in an awkward social situation by opening the conversation with a funny remark alluding to their condition. The ability of humor to aid those who must bear this kind of burden surely makes it among the greatest gifts of the human spirit.

The possible role of humor in dealing with another important medical problem should not be neglected. Mr Cousins mentioned the anesthetic effect of laughter in recounting the story of his illness, and there are other indications of an inverse relationship between humor and pain. One well-known anthropological study[3] compared the different styles of conceiving of and dealing with pain among patients of various ethnic backgrounds. The researchers discovered that among members of what he called the old

26

American population, it is widely believed that keeping one's sense of humor is an indispensable aid to coping with chronic pain. A physician I know would agree; he is often able to cure his patients' tension headaches simply by getting them to laugh at him!

Finally, the sense of humor has been linked—by long-standing tradition—with longevity. A doctor acquaintance of mine whose specialty is geriatric medicine has concluded that one thing which almost all his very healthy elderly patients seemed to have in common is a good sense of humor. Obviously, one must avoid drawing any inferences from such observations, for there are many unsolved mysteries about the aging process. Until they are unravelled, however, it remains a possibility that the mental attitude reflected in a lively sense of humor is an important factor predisposing some people toward long life.

As we have seen, observations suggest that there may be a positive relationship between good humor and good health. We need to go further than this, however. Ultimately, we need to bring these findings together into the broader framework of a preliminary explanatory scheme. This would help make the facts more intelligible and possibly even suggest further lines of investigation and discovery. Let us begin this quest by looking at some historical sources which lend support to these modern-day examples.

III

Humor and Health: The History of an Idea

Laughter and humor have long been thought to be health-giving. Beginning in ancient times, and continuing to the present day, there has been a long history of belief that a humorous outlook can both prevent and help cure disease. This idea is propounded in the Bible. Thus, in *Proverbs 17:22*, we are told: "A merry heart doeth good *like* a medicine: but a broken spirit drieth the bones."

This doctrine has also been espoused in the writing of scholars and medical men throughout the ages, and has been made the basis of systems of medical treatment in numerous cultural settings. Several modes of humor therapy seem to have enjoyed a vogue during the Middle Ages.

The great medieval professor of surgery, Henri de Mondeville, who lived from 1260 to 1320, was a proponent of mirth as an aid to recovery of surgical patients. In the classic treatise on his specialty, he writes "Let the surgeon take care to regulate the whole regimen of the patient's life for joy and happiness."[1]

Among the methods he recommends for accomplishing this goal are ". . . allowing his relatives and special friends to cheer him, and by having some one tell him jokes. . . . Keep up your patient's spirits by music of viols and ten-stringed psaltery."[2]

Finally, de Mondeville advises his readers that negative emotions must not be allowed to interfere with the patient's recovery. "The surgeon must forbid anger, hatred and sadness in the patient, and remind him that the body grows fat from joy and thin from sadness."[3]

Although it has its roots in an earlier era, the practice of keeping court fools or jesters is usually regarded as a medieval institution. Among the least-recognized functions of the jester was his role in maintaining (or even, at times, restoring) the physical or emotional health of the monarch. Will Somers, who served as court jester to King Henry VIII seems to be a case in point. The Shakespearean comic actor Robert Armin, describing Somers, relates:

> Leane he was, hollow eyde, as all report,
> And stoop he did, too; yet in all the court
> Few men were more belou'd then was this foole,
> Whose merry prate kept with the king much rule,
> When he was sad, the king and he would rime:
> Thus Will exiled sadness many a time.[4]

The jester Richard Tarlton, who served Queen Elizabeth I, apparently had the same knack. According to one account, Tarlton was

> . . . a master of his faculty. When Queen Elizabeth was serious, I dare not say sullen, and out of good humor, he could *undumpish* her at his pleasure. . . . He told the Queen . . . more of her faults than most of her chap-

lains; and cured her melancholy better than all her physicians.[5]

The most successful of the court fool-curers, however, seems to have been the Italian jester Bernardino (Il Matello) who was employed by Isabella d'Este late in the fifteenth century. When Isabella's brother Alfonso (who was, incidentally, the husband of the infamous Lucretia Borgia) fell ill, Isabella sent Matello to him to cheer him up. When, after several months, Alfonso sent the jester back home he sent with him an enthusiastic letter of thanks to his brother-in-law, in which he said:

> I truly believe that it is impossible for anyone to imagine the delight and the recreation and the pleasure that he, this buffoon, has afforded me, especially since he was the reason that, during his stay, the burden of my illness seemed lighter, even slight.[6]

Ironically, although Matello's bizarre humor eased the suffering of others in their times of sickness, it apparently complicated his own medical treatment during a serious illness. A doctor was charged by the jester's employers to cure him at any cost, but Matello greatly tried the patience of his physician. He steadfastly refused to take any of the prescribed medication and, through it all, kept on with his buffoonery.

Richard Mulcaster (1530–1611), an educator, recommended moderate laughter as an "exercise" which could be used for the benefit of pupils. Today, his notions, framed as they are in terms of an antiquated theory of medicine, themselves strike one as funny:

> But for *laughing* in the nature of an exercise and that healthful, can there be any better argument, to proue that it warmeth, then the rednesse of the face, and flush

30

of highe colour, when one laugheth from the hart and smiles not from the teethe? or that it stirreth the hart, and the adiacent partes, then the tickling and panting of those partes themselues? which both beare witnesse, that there is some quicke heat, that so moueth the blood. Therefore it must needs be good for them to vse *laughing,* which haue cold heades, and cold chestes, which are troubled with melancholie, which are light headed by reason of some cold distemperature of the braine, which thorough sadnesse, and sorrow, are subiecte to agues, which haue new dined, or supped; which are troubled with the head ache: for that a cold distemperature being the occasion of the infirmitie, *laughing* must needes helpe them, which moueth much aire in the breast, and sendeth the warmer spirites outward. This kinde of helpe wil be of much more efficacie, if the parties which desire it, can suffer themselues to be tickled vnder the armepittes, for in those partes there is great store of small veines, and litle arteries, which being tickled so, become warme themselues, and from thence disperse heat thorough out the whole bodie. But as moderate *laughing* is holesome, and maketh no too great chaunge, so to much is daungerous, and altereth to sore. . . . Besides this, no man wil denie, but that this kinde of *laughing* doth both much offende the head, and the bulke, as oftimes therewith both the papbones be loosed, and the backe it selfe perished. Nay what say ye to them that haue dyed *laughing?* where gladnesse of the minde to much enforcing the bodie, hath bereft it of life.[7]

When Robert Burton (1577–1640), an English parson and scholar, wrote his *Anatomy of Melancholy,* one of the earliest textbooks of psychiatry, he could cite a large number of learned authorities in support of laughter as a therapeutic measure. In writing of mirth as a cure for melancholy, he says:

Mirth and merry company may not be separated from music, both concerning and necessarily required in this business. "Mirth" (saith Vives) "purgeth the blood, confirms health, causeth a fresh, pleasing, and fine colour," prorogues life, whets the wit, makes the body young, lively, and fit for any manner of employment. The merrier the heart the longer the life; "A merry heart is the life of the flesh" (Prov.xiv,30); "Gladness prolongs his days" (Ecclus.xxx,22); and this is one of the three Salernitan doctors, Dr. Merryman, Dr. Diet, Dr. Quiet, which cures all diseases. . . . Gomesius . . . is a great magnifier of honest mirth, by which (saith he) "we cure many passions of the mind in ourselves, and in our friends". . . . Magninus holds, a merry companion is better than any music. . . . For these causes our physicians generally prescribe this as a principal engine to batter the walls of melancholy, a chief antidote, and a sufficient cure of itself. "By all means" (saith Mesue) "procure mirth to these men . . . to distract their minds from fear and sorrow, and such things on which they are so fixed and intent." "Let them use hunting, sports, plays, jests, merry company," as Rhasis prescribes, "which will not let the mind be molested, a cup of good drink now and then, hear music, and have such companions with whom they are especially delighted . . ." and by no means . . . suffer them to be alone. . . . to play the fool now and then is not amiss, there is a time for all things. This and many such means to exhilarate the heart of men have been still practiced in all ages, as knowing there is no better thing to the preservation of man's life. What shall I say then, but to every melancholy man,

Feast often, and use friends not still so sad,
Whose jests and merriments may make thee glad.

". . . Again and again I request you to be merry, if
anything trouble your hearts, or vex your souls, neglect
and contemn it, let it pass. And this I enjoin you, not as
a divine alone, but as a physician; for without this
mirth, which is the life and quintessence of physic,
medicines, and whatsoever is used and applied to pro-
long the life of man, is dull, dead, and of no force."
. . . Nothing better than mirth and merry company in
this malady. "It begins with sorrow" (saith Montanus),
"it must be expelled with hilarity."[8]

The German philosopher Immanuel Kant (1724–1804)
believed in effect, that laughter is a psychosomatic phenomenon; certain mental ideas result in a bodily response—
laughter—which has a beneficial physiological effect. He
explains his ideas on this subject in a section of his *Critique of
Judgment:*

"Music and that which excites laughter . . . give lively
gratification. . . . Thus we recognise pretty clearly that
the animation in both cases is merely bodily, although it
is excited by Ideas of the mind; and that the feeling of
health produced by a motion of the intestines corresponding to the play in question makes up that whole
gratification of a gay party, which is regarded as so
refined and so spiritual. It is not the judging the harmony in tones or sallies of wit, . . . but the furtherance
of the vital bodily processes, the affection that moves the
intestines and the diaphragm, in a word, the feeling of
health that makes up the gratification felt by us; so that
we can thus reach the body through the soul and use the
latter as the physician of the former. . . . In the case of
jokes, we feel the effect of this slackening in the body by

33

the oscillation of the organs, which promotes the resto-
ration of equilibrium and has a favorable influence
upon health. . . . Voltaire said that heaven had given us
two things to counterbalance the many miseries of life,
hope and sleep. He could have added laughter.[9]

Dr. William Battie, an English physician who is re-
nowned as an early proponent of medical treatment of the
mentally ill, put his sense of humor to work in his own
practice, as in the following story about him, related by
Dr. Doran, a nineteenth century historian:

> In the reign of George III, we have an instance of a
> professional man enacting the fool, with good intent
> and profitable purpose. The person alluded to is the
> learned and laughter-loving Dr. William Battie, who
> was well-reputed London physician in portions of the
> reigns of George II and his successor. He was celebrated
> for his treatment of the insane; and is thus described in
> the *Battiad,* a poem of which he was the hero,

> "First Battas came, deep read in wordly art,
> Whose tongue ne'er knew the secrets of his heart.
> In mischief mighty, though but mean of size,
> And, like the Tempter, ever in disguise.
> See him with aspect grave and gentle tread,
> By slow degrees approach the sickly bed;
> Then, at his club, behold him alter'd soon,
> The solemn doctor turns a low buffoon."

But Battie could play the fool, even to better purpose by
the sick bed, than the buffoon at his club. It is told of
him that he had a young male patient whom obstinate
quinsy* threatened with almost instant suffocation.

* Quinsy is an abscess in the region of the tonsils, and is caused by an
infection by Streptococcal bacteria, the organisms which are found in strep
throat.

Battie had tried every remedy but his foolery, and at last he had recourse to *that.* Setting his wig wrong side before, twisting his face into a compound comic expression, and darting his head suddenly within the curtains, he cut such antics, poured forth such delicious folly, and was altogether so irresistible, that his patient, after gazing at him for a moment in stupefaction, burst into a fit of laughter which broke the imposthume,* and rescued the sufferer from impending death.[10]

James Sully, who published a comprehensive book on laughter in the early part of the twentieth century, extols the physiological benefits conferred by laughter:

What truth is there in the saying that laughter has beneficial physiological effects? . . . To begin with, the unlearned, have had a shrewd conviction that laughter sets the current of life moving briskly. Proverbs, such as "laugh and grow fat," attest this common conviction. Those who have catered to the laughter-lovers have not unnaturally made much of this salutary influence. . . . This popular view has been supported by the weight of learned authority. Vocal exercises, of which laughing is clearly one, have been recommended by experts as a means of strengthening the lungs and of furthering the health of the organism as a whole. By many, moreover, laughter has been specifically inculcated as a hygienic measure. . . . Both by a vigorous reinforcement of the actions of the large muscles which do the work of respiration, and, still more, by the beneficial effects of these reinforced actions on the functions of the lungs and the circulatory apparatus, laughter properly finds a place among "bodily exercizes." . . . How far these

---

* Imposthume is an archaic word for abscess. Dr. Battie wasn't aware of the role of bacteria in this disease. If he were practicing today, he would supplement his laughter therapy with penicillin.

benign effects on health, which are recognised by the modern physician as well as by his predecessor, are due to the vigorous reinforcement brought by laughter to the work of respiration and of the circulation of the blood it is not easy to say. . . . At the same time we must not lose sight of the possibility that laughter may act beneficially on our hard-pressed frames in another way. As has been suggested above, the lusty cachinnation is nature's way of voicing gladness, a sudden increase of pleasure. Now it has been held by psychologists that pleasurable feelings tend to further the whole group of organic functions, by adding to the nervous vigour which keeps them going. Laughter may owe a part of its benign influence on our bodily state to the fact that it produces a considerable increase of vital activity by way of heightened nervous stimulation.[11]

William McDougall, at one time a professor of psychology at Harvard, wrote an article proposing that the very biological function of laughter was one of helping to maintain psychological health and well-being. He saw it as a built-in regulatory mechanism which prevents the tendency toward sympathy, which is necessary for civilized and social life among men, from making man's mental state one of constant depression. He noted that laughter has two effects on the laugher:

First, laughter interrupts the train of mental activity; it diverts or rather relaxes the attention, and so prevents the further play of the mind upon the ludicrous object. . . . Secondly, the bodily movements of laughter hasten the circulation and respiration and raise the blood pressure; and so bring about a condition of *euphoria* or general well-being which gives a pleasurable tone to consciousness.

36

We are now in a position to see what laughter does for us, what advantages we gain from the possession of the capacity for laughter as a part of our native endowment. The possession of this peculiar disposition shields us from the depressing influence which the many minor mishaps and shortcomings of our fellows would exert upon us if we did not possess it. . . . It not only prevents our minds from dwelling upon these depressing objects, but it actually converts these objects into stimulants that promote our well-being, both bodily and mentally, instead of depressing us through sympathetic pain or distress. *Laughter is primarily and fundamentally the antidote of sympathetic pain.* The sympathetic tendencies are of the first importance for the life of society. . . . But though it was of importance that we should sympathetically share the enjoyments of our fellows, and feel something of their more serious distresses; it would have been a serious disadvantage to the species, if each man had had to suffer sympathetically all the minor pains of his fellows; for these minor pains were so abundantly spread around him that he would have been almost continuously subjected to their depressing influence, and, under the cumulative effect of so many slight pains, his vitality would have been seriously lowered. Hence, some antidote, some preventive of these too frequent, and useless, minor sympathetic pains became necessary; therefore, the capacity for laughter was acquired as a protective reaction against them.[12]

Probably the most enthusiastic defense of the role of laughter in health ever written is the book *Laughter and Health,* published in 1928 by the American physician, James J. Walsh. Walsh suggests that the health-giving effect of laughter derives primarily from a mechanical, stimulating effect on

37

the internal organs of the body, although he also allows for the importance of certain psychological and attitudinal factors:

> The best formula for the health of the individual is contained in the mathematical expression health varies as the amount of laughter. . . .
>
> While laughter is a mystery from its mental aspect, it is easy to appreciate its far-reaching physical effects. The diaphragm, the principal organ involved in it, is in intimate anatomical relations with all the organs in the body that carry on the physical life. Whenever there are convulsive movements in the diaphragm, they are sure to be affected by them. As laughter always makes us feel better for having indulged in it, it is evident that the effect of the movements of the diaphragm and the large organs in its neighborhood is beneficial.
>
> . . . There seems no doubt that hearty laughter stimulates practically all the large organs, and by making them do their work better through the increase of circulation that follows the vibratory massage which accompanies it, heightens resistive vitality against disease. Besides, the mental effect brushes away the dreads and fears which constitute the basis of so many diseases or complaints and lifts men out of the slough of despond into which they are so likely to fall when they take themselves overseriously.
>
> Laughter makes one expansive in outlook and is very likely to give the feeling that the future need not be the subject of quite so much solicitude as is usually allowed for it.
>
> The effect of laughter upon the mind not only brings relaxation with it, so far as mental tension is concerned, but makes it also less prone to dreads and less

38

solicitous about the future. This favorable effect on the mind influences various functions of the body and makes them healthier than would otherwise be the case.[13]

Nor have such beliefs and practices been confined to the Western cultural and scientific tradition. Numerous American Indian tribes, including the Pueblo, Hopi, Zuni, and Cree, had orders of ceremonial clowns who were charged with the important role of provoking mirth among their fellow tribesmen. They entertained, just as their counterparts in our own society do, by their weird dress and outrageous behavior. They served other essential social functions as well, including, oddly, that of policemen, maintaining order during certain ceremonial occasions. For our present purposes, the most important of these other roles was that of curing. The clown-doctors of the Plains Ojibway were called the *windigokan*. Their traditional license to engage in hilarity was so complete that it extended even to their behavior when they were called in to heal the sick.

> When a sick person's case had been diagnosed by the doctor or seer as one of infection by disease demons, word was sent to the leader of the windigokan who brought his troop into the patient's lodge where they danced before the invalid, pounding their rattles on the ground, singing, whistling, and dancing. They approached, looked at the sufferer, started back, ran away, and reapproached with all manner of grotesque and fantastic actions, until the demons of ill health had been frightened away.[14]

So, there has been a long tradition of folk belief, and a long line of scholarship in support of it, to the effect that laughter is good for health. However, there are reasons for believing that the matter is not that simple. In the first place, what is lacking in the historical sources is a clear-cut explanation as to why mirth is so beneficial. In addition, as we shall see in the next three chapters, humor and laughter can also be intimately associated with disease.

IV

Laughter and Disease

There are times when laughter isn't so funny, when it is not an indicator of health, but a sign of disease. At first, it may seem strange to say that there can be sicknesses involving laughter, or illnesses affecting the sense of humor, but in fact there are many. This is an important reality of medicine for a number of reasons, not the least of which is that it enables the doctor to use observations of a patient's mirth diagnostically. Diagnosis is one of the most important tasks of the physician, since accurate diagnosis is essential in order that the doctor may determine what specific therapy is appropriate for the patient. So, the fact that characteristic dysfunctions of humor and laughter are part of the patterns of numerous organic diseases of the nervous system is significant in that it gives the doctor yet another guideline in the attempt to figure out exactly what is wrong with the patient.

A single, distinctive type of aberrant laughter is found in three neurological disorders: pseudobulbar palsy, amyotrophic lateral sclerosis, and multiple sclerosis. Pseudobulbar palsy is a condition which is most frequently caused by a series of infarctions or strokes involving both hemispheres of the cerebrum of the brain. Persons with this disorder are usually unable to speak clearly—their speech sounds garbled and indistinct—and they have difficulty swallowing. In addition, they may suffer from the paralysis of their arms or legs, or one or both sides of the body. Sudden outbursts of uncontrolled laughter are so typical a feature of pseudobulbar palsy that at one time it was actually called "the laughing disease."

This same condition is also frequently a part of the picture in the exceedingly tragic disease known as amyotrophic lateral sclerosis (ALS), or Lou Gehrig's disease, after the famous American baseball player who suffered from it. ALS, which for some unknown reason is more commonly found in males than in females, is almost invariably a disease of middle age or later life. It may first appear quite innocuous; the patient may complain simply of pain in his legs. It later becomes apparent, however, that the leg muscles are painful because he has been unknowingly working them harder just to get around, for they are getting steadily weaker. This weakness gradually worsens and spreads to other parts of the body. Eventually, when it involves muscles in the face, palate, throat and tongue, he becomes unable to speak clearly, or to swallow, and he must be fed through a tube.

The shrivelling muscles of the body, as they grow weaker and weaker, fasciculate—that is, twitch uncontrollably— sometimes to such a marked degree that large areas of the body's musculature give the appearance of an undulating surface. Often these patients, near the end, are subject to intense outbursts of laughter which they cannot control. The course of this disease, unfortunately, is relentless, and there is no known treatment or cure. Its victims grow steadily weaker until they die, usually from a respiratory infection which, due to their debilitated and malnourished state, their bodies are unable to resist.

It is known that the basic problem in ALS is that the nerve cells in the spinal cord and brain stem which control the movements of the muscles begin to degenerate, and that this in turn causes the muscles themselves to weaken and then atrophy. What is still unknown, however, is why the nerve cells begin to deteriorate in this way. Some have suggested that a nutritional disturbance may be involved, while others suggest factors such as infections or even poisons.

Another disease of unknown etiology, multiple sclerosis (MS), in many ways contrasts sharply with ALS, since it is primarily a disease of young adults, and seems more frequently to affect women than men, again for reasons unknown. Furthermore, although it is generally progressive over a long duration, it is characterized by marked exacerbations or flare-ups, followed by the patient's improvement for a time, sometimes even for long periods. Indeed, people with MS often live for many years—even decades—with their disorder. In addition, multiple sclerosis has a baffling geographical predilection; for some reason, it is almost nonexistent in tropical or sub-tropical areas, but in areas with colder climates the incidence goes up sharply.

The pattern of symptoms in this disease is quite perplexing. The patient's initial difficulty may be a visual disturbance: She may state that she sees double, or has an area of blindness in the visual field, or has blurred vision. Later, weakness of the legs and, less frequently, of the arms sets in. But the degree of weakness actually present varies widely among different patients. They experience trouble in

43

coordinating the movement of their arms, and appear quite clumsy in trying to accomplish rather simple tasks.

In a significant percentage of persons with this disease, bizarre, subjective changes of the state of consciousness take place—changes which patients say are very difficult, or impossible, to describe or to explain to others. In addition, MS patients are frequently very buoyant in mood, almost euphoric. Visitors to the hospital often remark how cheerful they seem despite the grave nature of their disease.

The pathological changes in the nervous system which are associated with MS affect a fatty substance known as myelin. Myelin is layered around the long fibers of nerve cells and has the function of lowering the resistance of these fibers so that the electrical impulses conveying information in the nervous system can travel faster. In multiple sclerosis, this myelin degenerates. So far, no one has explained why it begins to do so, though some believe that a poorly-understood virus or allergic response may be involved. Unfortunately, at present there is no way permanently to reverse or to halt this deterioration of the myelin, although steroid drugs are of some benefit to the patients during the flare-ups.

Despite the many contrasts between ALS and MS, in one important point they are similar. For, the victims of multiple sclerosis, too, are subject to the same episodic bouts of pathological, irresistable laughter.

As mentioned earlier, the laughter which is a feature of the three diseases just described has its own distinctive characteristics. In one way, it is like normal laughter; specifically, the patient is generally fully conscious of its occurring, and remembers having laughed afterwards. In many other respects, though, it is unlike healthy laughter. For instance, this

44

aberrant mirth is not under the control of the patient. He does not will it; it simply happens to him, and he may be unable to stop it. Once it does start, it tends to be prolonged; it may last for several minutes, and attacks of it may occur many times daily. It is often followed by unpleasant, or distressing physiological after-effects: The patient's heart rate may go up, or he may have difficulty breathing normally. There is also a tendency for this laughter to be associated, in the same individuals, with similarly uncontrolled and extended attacks of weeping.

Most importantly, though, this forced laughter is unlike normal mirth in that it is not a manifestation of the true mood of the patient. He may say, in fact, that he does not feel joyful or happy at all; he just laughs, spontaneously. The laughter may at times be set off by an appropriately funny remark or incident, but once it starts, it proceeds on its own, and no appropriate feeling is present behind it. The seeming exception to this statement posed by the buoyant mood of the multiple sclerosis patient is only apparent; for the euphoric mood and the uncontrollable laughter are separate phenomena in this condition, with distinct causes.

However, a very interesting psychological effect sometimes occurs in this type of laughter. Patients may report that, after a long and vigorous bout of forced laughter, their mood will, in effect, follow along. That is, while they do not feel joyful when the attack begins, as it proceeds they feel within themselves an awakening sense of mirth. These same considerations apply to the aberrant weeping found in these three diseases. Initially, it does not represent a mood of sadness, but may, if lengthy and severe, provoke such a mood.

A similar kind of pathological laughter occasionally

accompanies a certain hereditary disease—Wilson's disease. In this condition, however, the picture is even more complicated due to the presence of unusual psychological manifestations.

If you will look very closely some time at the labels of your high-potency vitamin and mineral pills, you may see, in tiny print, a statement to the effect that patients with Wilson's disease should avoid that preparation. The reason behind this warning is quite interesting. Copper, one of the minerals present in the capsule, is a necessary component of the diet of the normal person. Human beings must obtain minute quantities of copper from their diet, because it plays a vital role in certain metabolic processes in the body.

However, persons with Wilson's disease have an inherited deficiency of the chemical substance which, in normal individuals, serves to carry copper through the bloodstream. Consequently, in this disease, the patient's body is slowly but progressively poisoned by the small traces of copper present in the normal human diet. Instead of being distributed properly, the copper is deposited in the bodily tissues, particularly in the liver, where its gradual accumulation over the years causes the liver to shrink and to form nodules, ultimately resulting in the symptoms of cirrhosis.

Unusual changes in pigmentation, discoloration of the skin or other tissues, caused by the deposition of copper compounds, may be present as well. For, instance, areas of the nails may show a pale bluish color, and there may be a greenish ring around the iris of the eye, in the region where it joins the sclera, or white part of the eye.

The accumulating copper damages the nervous system, too, resulting in symptoms such as the so-called wing flapping tremor, a peculiar, involuntary, beating movement of the arms. Patients are sometimes prone to wide, drastic swings of mood, and some complain of uncontrolled smiling and forced laughter as an annoying feature of their condition. Some clinicians, in describing Wilson's disease, have mentioned that patients occasionally have a fixed, silly expression on their faces, as if their features were frozen into a facetious grin. Due to these unusual emotional manifestations, it sometimes happens that a young person who appears for the first time with these symptoms is misdiagnosed as being schizophrenic; later it turns out that the correct diagnosis is Wilson's disease.

The initial signs of Wilson's disease tend to show up rather early in life. If it is diagnosed quickly enough, the institution of therapeutic measures can minimize the harm which would otherwise result from the untreated disease. The amount of copper in the patient's diet can be carefully regulated. Also, a drug is available which, administered with meals, prevents the copper in food from being absorbed from the gastrointestinal tract. Another medication can be used to increase the excretion of copper by the kidneys.

Disordered laughter of an unusual kind may occur as a manifestation, sometimes even the sole manifestation, of epilepsy. Typically, the parents of a child with this disorder will bring him to the doctor, stating that once in a while the child, without any obvious provocation, suddenly begins to laugh. The parents may describe the laughter as dull, hollow, inappropriate. The attack may be coupled with other epileptic symptoms; the child may fall down, or jerk, concurrently with the laughter. This epileptic laughter lacks the contagious quality of normal, happy mirth; the patient may

47

deny that he feels joyful during the laughing spells or may even say that, afterwards, he doesn't remember them at all. Fortunately, in many cases, these so-called "gelastic fits" can be prevented by regular use of the medications with which, in recent times, we have succeeded so well in bringing epilepsy under control.

Kuru is perhaps the weirdest of the organic diseases in which one routinely finds abnormal laughter.[1] Quite fortunately for the rest of us, this illness is confined to a very small corner of the world, certain highland areas of New Guinea, where it occurs only among members of the Fore tribe. Kuru, which is also known by the ghastly name "the laughing death," begins insidiously with tremors and incoordination and progresses invariably to death. Uncontrolled, hilarious and uproarious laughter is a very bad prognostic sign, signifying that the terminal stage has arrived.

Cultural factors are closely interwoven into the picture of kuru, for the tribesmen believe it to be caused by a kind of witchcraft. Relatives of someone who had died of kuru will try to find out who was responsible for the inimical spell and, if they do decide who did it, will murder him in retaliation. Interestingly, people who are afflicted seem to derive a great deal of humorous pleasure out of their own inability to coordinate their movements. They laugh at their awkward gait, at their slurred speech, and at their failure to perform simple tasks. Other, non-afflicted members of the community—even friends and relatives of the dying person—join in the hilarity and good fun, teasing and laughing.

Researchers who have investigated the disease believe, on various grounds, that it is an infection of an unusual type which does not cause the ordinary consequences of infections, such as fever. The infectious agent is believed to be a virus with a unique mode of transmission. The Fore tribesmen are cannibals, and evidence suggests that the virus is spread by the ritual ingestion of brain tissue. Fortunately, now that the tribe has been influenced by Western customs and prohibitions, the practice of cannibalism is being obliterated, and kuru, which was formerly one of the primary causes of death among these preliterate people, is gradually vanishing.

Poisoning or intoxication by a number of drugs or chemical substances can result in excessive, uncontrolled or inappropriate laughter. In our society, ethyl alcohol is the most widely known and abused of these substances. Some say that persons acutely intoxicated with alcohol go through distinct stages. At first, they seem gay, happy, joking and laughing. They are clownish—albeit the kind of clownishness that they usually regret the next day, when the party is over. Later, they may become sad, despondent, and despairing. Then, they sometimes grow belligerent or angry, and may provoke a fight. Finally, they collapse into an unresponsive state and lose consciousness. In medical school, we learned to memorize this sequence by a mnemonic device: "jocose, morose, bellicose, comatose."

Alcohol is known to act as a depressant of the central nervous system. In light of the experiment described in Chapter I, in which stimulants seem to increase the appreciation of humor and depressants to decrease it, it may seem hard to explain why alcohol may bring about increased mirth. The answer to this appears to be that the early depressant effect of alcohol is on the processes which normally act to inhibit behavior which the person regards as socially unacceptable. So, paradoxically, his inhibitions are loosened

49

up, and a humorous streak which he normally keeps in check is revealed to us.

Yet another drug which is associated with easy laughter is marijuana. Persons under its influence frequently report that hilarious mirth is set off by remarks or happenings that in the situation seem quite amusing, although they wouldn't have seemed at all funny under normal circumstances.

Laughter is so well-known a side-effect of one anesthetic agent that this fact has given the drug its popular name. Nitrous oxide, also called "laughing gas," was one of the first agents employed to abolish the pain of surgery. As a matter of fact, its propensity to provoke great gales of laughter was recognized and employed on a grand scale even before it was widely used as a pain-killer.

During the 1840's a man by the name of Colton succeeded in commercializing the instant jubilation available through the inhalation of this gas. He made the rounds of the villages and cities of New England with a traveling show, the likes of which hasn't been seen in America before or since. At his stops, he would assemble the townspeople and dispense the gas to them for twenty-five cents a whiff. For an engagement in Connecticut, he distributed a most interesting handbill to announce his exhibition:

> A Grand Exhibition of the effects produced by inhaling Nitrous Oxid, Exhilarating or Laughing Gas! will be given at Union Hall this (Tuesday) Evening, Dec. 10th, 1844.

> Forty gallons of Gas will be prepared and administered to all in the audience who desire to inhale it.

> Twelve Young Men have volunteered to inhale the Gas, to commence the entertainment.

Eight Strong Men are engaged to occupy the front seats to protect those under the influence of the Gas from injuring themselves or others. This course is adopted that no apprehension of danger may be entertained. Probably no one will attempt to fight.

The effect of the Gas is to make those who inhale it either Laugh, Sing, Dance, Speak or Fight, and so forth, according to the leading trait of their character. They seem to retain consciousness enough not to say or do that which they would have occasion to regret.

N.B.—The Gas will be administered only to gentlemen of the first respectability. The object is to make the entertainment in every respect a genteel affair.[2]

Poisoning with the metal manganese also brings about aberrations of laughter. This kind of poisoning is confined entirely to those whose day-to-day work has to do with the production or use of the element. It is found most commonly among manganese miners,[3] but occasionally among persons employed in the assembly of dry cell batteries as well.

Generally, exposure occurs when the dust is inhaled. After a time, those poisoned are plagued with headaches, and a morbid inability to stay alert; they appear constantly drowsy and tired. Over a period of time, these symptoms worsen, and patients may begin to experience nightmarish visions. A recognizable and distinct distortion of the facial expression—a facetious, silly grin—is so characteristic of this illness that it has acquired the name "manganese mask." The waves of laughter which the patients experience seem appropriate to their mood, for it is reported that they are continually euphoric. Interestingly, their laughter is, like normal laughter, quite contagious. If several victims of the disorder are assembled, the laughter of one of them will set off a wave of reverberating guffaws affecting them all. Nonetheless, the laughter strikes observers as inappropriate and excessive, in that seemingly insignificant jokes or remarks will set off relatively immense jags of laughter.

The phrase "sardonic laughter" has come to mean a sneering, cynical laughter of derision, or, in the words of Dr. Samuel Johnson, "a distortion of the face without gladness of heart." Originally, however, the term was coined to designate a kind of pathological laughter brought on by poisoning. Numerous ancient writers wrote of a poisonous plant which grew in Sardinia. Persons who ingested it were stricken with convulsive, unwilled laughter, which terminated only in death. From this came the phrase "Sardinian laughter," or *risus sardonicus,* and this terrible laughter is seen even today in two well-known toxic conditions.

Strychnine poisoning is regrettably still a problem on rare occasions. Now and then, children unknowingly consume rodent poisons containing the compound. There are also occasional poisonings among religious cultists who try to demonstrate their faith by deliberately consuming the substance in preparations called "salvation cocktails."

Strychnine acts upon the body by stimulating the central nervous system. Victims are plagued by intense convulsions; their respiration is severely compromised and, due to the engorgement of blood in their veins, they turn a frightening blue-black color. They remain acutely conscious, but their sense of orientation is overwhelmed; they have the feeling of being tossed through space by uncontrolled forces. During the entire episode of the strychnine convulsion, they have a feeling of oncoming doom. The spasms of the facial muscles impart to the face the horrifying, grin-like *risus sardonicus* expression.

52

The *risus sardonicus* is also seen in tetanus ("lockjaw"). In this disease, the spasms of the face muscles are caused by a poisonous agent released by infecting bacteria which may gain entrance to the body through a dirty wound.

Having now surveyed the major toxic conditions which may be accompanied by unnatural laughter, we shall go on to look into three other conditions which bear upon our present topic. In these states—the pre-senile dementias, Kleine-Levin syndrome, and mirth-related deaths—there are even more striking and incomprehensible abnormalities of mirth than we have encountered up to now.

A highly unusual disorder of the sense of humor occurs in patients who are afflicted with the so-called "pre-senile dementias." Dementia is, to put it simply, a loss of intellectual functioning, and we have come to associate this process with the gradual encroachment of old age. However, in pre-senile dementias, called Alzheimer's disease and Pick's disease, senility appears to come on prematurely, sometimes even when the patient is in his or her forties. Degenerative changes, the causes and mechanism of which are unknown, begin to take place in the patient's brain, and proceed at a greatly accelerated rate. The outward effect is that the person seems to become old, very rapidly. This may first be manifested as a change in recent memory; the patient is unable to recall what happened yesterday, or this morning, though events of earlier life are remembered with greater ease.

The defect in the sense of humor present in these conditions is known as moria. This is a kind of facetiousness, a tendency to crack silly jokes and an inability to take serious matters seriously. The patient's behavior is very inappropriate to his situation; it is almost as though he is not aware—or is unable to become aware—of how grave and unfortunate his illness is. Observing his incessant, impenetrable jocularity, one almost receives the impression that he is using his facetious manner as a psychological defense against becoming aware of what is happening to his mind.

Kleine-Levin syndrome is a rare, mysterious disorder of sleep, nutrition, and mental functioning which affects only adolescent males. In this condition, patients become ravenously hungry, or, at least, begin to eat excessively. They stuff themselves with food, snatching it from the plate even as it is being served to them, and wolfing it down. After a prolonged bout of eating everything in sight, they become somnolent. They sometimes sleep for days, periodically awakening only to go to the bathroom.

Klein-Levin syndrome is a paroxysmal disorder. It tends to come on in attacks from which the patient recovers after a few days or weeks; this is followed by a long period of respite during which he does not have any symptoms. Then, weeks or months later, without warning, a subsequent attack takes place.

During the episodes, the patient's behavior may seem almost psychotic. Prominent among the psychological symptoms are strange eccentricities in the sense of humor or laughter. In one of the classical articles on Kleine-Levin syndrome,[4] it was noted that one patient laughed compulsively and uncontrollably during one of his attacks. Yet another patient was described as going into self-imposed isolation on the ward and performing—by and for himself—comic routines that Charlie Chaplin had made famous in his movies. It was also reported that another patient, as he was recovering from one bout with the illness, became inexplicably preoccupied with an urgent and morbid desire to play practical jokes.

The cause of this curious malady is unknown, and no treatment is available, other than that of hospitalizing and watching the patient during these periodic crises, so that he will not harm himself or others. In light of the fact that the disorder cannot be cured, it is good to know that Kleine-Levin syndrome eventually takes care of itself. As the patient's adolescent period draws to a close, his condition goes away of its own accord, leaving him with no lasting harmful effects, disappearing just as mysteriously as it appeared.

It will perhaps be appropriate to bring this chapter to a close by citing some instances which suggest that the phrase "I could die laughing" may sometimes be more than mere hyperbole. For, some sources describe cases in which death from—or at least during—violent, excessive laughter, has taken place. One nineteenth-century medical text mentions numerous cases of "death from violent laughter" drawn from both classical and modern writings, but the authors are of the opinion that, in these events, ". . . it is very probable that death was not due to the emotion itself, but to the extreme convulsion and exertion used in the laughter."[5]

These same physicians go on to call attention to an abominable method of execution by laughter allegedly employed by members of a sixteenth-century Protestant sect. "Strange as it may seem, Saint-Foix says that the Moravian brothers, a sect of Anabaptists having great horror of bloodshed, executed their condemned brethren by tickling them to death."[6]

In an article describing their own research into laughter, two psychologists described yet another instance, one in which overwhelming psychological factors were also of great importance.

55

A frontiersman, in a well authenticated case, came home to find his dearly beloved wife and children all lying dead, scalped and mutilated by Indians. He burst out into a fit of laughter, exclaiming repeatedly, "It is the funniest thing I ever heard of," and laughed on convulsively and uncontrollably till he died from a ruptured blood vessel.[7]

Yet another psychologist relates how gladiators who suffered fatal wounds involving the diaphragm during battles in the arena would be overcome, as they were dying, with paroxysms of laughter.[8] He concludes that this was a reflex phenomenon, rather than a result of specific psychological stress.

In summary, then, we have seen that one must not be too quick to accept the now all too apparently over-simplified concept of the relationship between health and laughter embodied in Walsh's equation, "The best formula for the health of the individual is contained in the mathematical expression: health varies as the amount of laughter."[9] For, there are cases in which laughter can be closely linked to disease, too. We have seen, indeed, that—in what must be one of life's supreme ironies—laughter can be an ominous harbinger of impending death.

However, in terms of common sense, although it seems extremely unnatural to associate laughter with organic disease, it somehow seems quite natural to associate laughter with mental illness. It is to this striking fact that we will now turn our attention.

V

Laughter and Madness

The ancient Greek physician Hippocrates, the father of modern medicine, left to us through his writings a legacy of sound clinical observation and judgment, much of which is relevant and valuable even today, over two thousand years later. The story of his encounter with the philosopher Democritus is germane to our topic: Heraclitus the philosopher had fallen into a deep depression because of his serious contemplation of the sad lot of humanity. He wept and railed against heaven for the foolishness, pain, and insanity of his fellow human beings. Democritus, on the other hand, in response to similar thoughts, laughed at humanity's foolishness, useless pain, and general insanity. The people of his native town of Abdera thought he was mad, and sending emissaries to Hippocrates, pleaded that the famous physician not delay in curing their townsman.

When Hippocrates arrived in Abdera, the citizens surrounded him, some in tears of sorrow, some in tears of gratitude, some begging that he do his best. Robert Burton picks up the story here:

> After some little repast, he went to see Democritus, the
> people following him, whom he found (as before) in his

garden. . . . Hippocrates, after a little pause, saluted him. . . . Hippocrates commended his work, admiring his happiness and leisure. "And why," quoth Democritus, "have not you that leisure?" "Because," replied Hippocrates, "domestical affairs hinder necessary to be done for ourselves, neighbors, friends; expenses, diseases, frailties and mortalities which happen; wife, children, servants, and such businesses which deprive us of our time." At this speech Democritus profusely laughed (his friends and the people standing by, weeping in the meantime and lamenting his madness.) Hippocrates asked the reason why he laughed. He told him, "At the vanities and the fopperies of the time, to see men so empty of all virtuous actions, to hunt so far after gold, having no end of ambition; to take such infinite pains for a little glory, and to be favoured of men; to make such deep mines into the earth for gold, and many times to find nothing, with loss of their lives and fortunes. . . . Do not these behaviours express their intolerable folly? When men live in peace, they covet war, detesting quietness, deposing kings, and advancing others in their stead. . . . When they are poor and needy, they seek riches, and when they have them, they do not enjoy them, but hide them underground, or else wastefully spend them. O wise Hippocrates, I laugh at such things being done, but much more when no good comes of them, and when they are done to so ill purpose. There is no truth or justice found amongst them for they daily plead one against another, the son against the father and the mother, brother against brother, kindred and friends of the same quality; and all this for riches, whereof after death they cannot be possessors. And yet, notwithstanding, they will defame and kill one another, commit all unlawful actions contemning God and men, friends and country. They make great account of many senseless things, esteeming them as a great part of their treasure, statues, pictures and such-like movables, dear-bought, and so cunningly wrought, as nothing but speech wanteth in them, and yet they hate living persons speaking to them. Others affect difficult things; if they dwell on firm land they will move to an island, and thence to land again, being no way constant to their desires. They commend courage and strength in wars, and let themselves be conquered by lust and avarice. . . . And now, methinks, O most worthy Hippocrates, you should not reprehend my laughing, perceiving so many fooleries in men; for no man will mock his own folly, but that which he seeth in a second, and so they justly mock one another. . . . Seeing men are so fickle, so sottish, so intemperate, why should not I laugh at those to whom folly seems wisdom, will not be cured, and perceive it not?"

It grew late: Hippocrates left him; and no sooner was he come away, but all the citizens came about flocking, to know how he liked him. He told them in brief, that notwithstanding those small neglects of his attire, body, diet, the world had not a wiser, a more learned, a more honest man, and they were much deceived to say that he was mad.[1]

Now, the story above clearly illustrates two points. We will defer discussion of the second point until the end of this chapter, but the first point is this: Ages ago, just as today, inappropriate or excessive laughter was regarded in the popular mind as a sign of madness. Charles Baudelaire, the nineteenth century French poet, epitomized this attitude with his remark: "Laughter is one of the most frequent signs of madness."[2] Nor can the practical ramifications of this conception be ignored. One of the worries expressed by patients suffering from some of the organic diseases of the nervous system discussed in the previous chapter is that others will conclude, because of their uncontrolled laughter, that they are crazy.

This belief has infused itself into the very language with which we describe and evaluate mental disorder. There is an astounding degree of overlap in ordinary language between the words which are used to describe behavior as mentally disturbed and those which are used to describe behavior as humorous. This ambiguity extends even to the word "funny" itself. "Funny behavior" could just as easily mean disturbed behavior as it could amusing behavior. Comic individuals, actions, or incidents are typically characterized as "dizzy," "zany," "mad," "goofy," "daffy," "crazy," "wild," "hysterical," "insane," "madcap," and so on. These same labels are used at times in informal conversation to characterize actions or thoughts as mentally disturbed. In the late 1950's, the term "sick joke" was coined to denote a variety of humor then in vogue which, one feels, would only be thought funny by someone who was emotionally disturbed—who was, to be more specific, sadistic.

The significance of such associations can hardly be overrated. Indeed, the interplay between those two notions—the mad and the funny—has been a continual source of fascination for the human mind in life, in literature, and in science.

Dramatists, poets, and novelists have produced an unending series of literary works in which the "fool"—the madman, retarded person, or professional comedian—has been portrayed, paradoxically, as the mouthpiece of wisdom and truth. A character drawn from real life has been moulded by creative artists into a symbolic spokesman for profound philosophical puzzles concerning life and reality, and for paradoxes about the nature of mad versus "normal" behavior. Shakespeare, for instance, made powerful and inspired use of this technique in *King Lear*.

It is not to be imagined, however, that the association between mental illness and funniness is a peculiarity only of the non-medical public or of the poetic imagination. It also permeates the professional literature of psychology, psychiatry, and medicine. Just as playwrights have appropriated the character of the madman from real life and used him for dramatic ends, the reverse movement has taken place as well. Thus, the clown, a creation of the actor and of the dramatist's fancy, presumably with no place in "real," everyday life, has been used as a descriptive device to characterize the behavior of the insane. Karl Kahlbaum, the psychiatrist who first described catatonic schizophrenia, wrote of the "clownishness" of patients with mania.[3]

Even in the most recent textbooks of psychiatry, various recognized mental disorders are described or defined by the use of some of the very same terms that are used to characterize people, events, or remarks as funny, humorous, or laughter-provoking. In a number of texts, passages describing the behavior of persons with some mental disorders abound with words like "ludicrous," "silly," "whimsical," "absurd," "ridiculous," and "jocular."

In crueler and less enlightened eras, such associations were perverted to the extreme. Thus, at one time mental patients were put on public display for the amusement and laughter of the public, even in institutions supposedly estab-

61

lished to care for them. Madmen and retarded persons were kept as court fools during ancient and medieval periods, so that the ruler and his retinue could revel in their hilarity.

Today, we are aghast at the very idea that such things were ever done. Our sense of shock should serve to remind us of a very important point: The symptomatic similarities of humor and madness do not imply that psychosis is a funny matter, or that one can feel justified in laughing at psychotics. Indeed, the exact reverse is true. For psychosis is among the most unfunny of human dilemmas, in that it involves the most extreme and acute kind of human suffering, while psychotics themselves can, of all persons, be among the most highly sensitive to being laughed at.

This points to an extremely crucial distinction—one, it is hoped, which reflects a real social advance. There is a great difference between a society's allowing or encouraging abusive or heartless laughter at madmen, on the one hand, and the practice of using labels like "ridiculous" and "ludicrous" in textbook characterizations of mental illness, on the other. Such terms are intended in these texts not to ridicule or to make fun of patients, but to describe them, and, hence, to aid the physician in the goal of diagnosing and, ultimately, of treating and helping his patients.

The textbook descriptions to which I have alluded are helpful guides to diagnosis in part because of the fact that specific and characteristic dysfunctions of mirth are prominent features of numerous mental or emotional illnesses, including depression, schizophrenia, paranoid states, mania, and hysteria. This is so obviously true with respect to some of those conditions that it hardly needs to be mentioned. For instance, severely depressed persons often show a marked deficiency of laughter, smiling, or mirth. In other instances, though, the association is not so much a matter of common knowledge.

Schizophrenia, which was once called dementia prae-cox, is actually a family of mental illnesses characterized by a loss of contact with reality, auditory and visual hallucinations, and severe disturbances of thinking and feeling. Schizophrenia has long been associated with a certain kind of inappropriate laughter, even by the clinicians who first classified it. Emil Kraepelin, an influential figure in the development of modern psychiatry, wrote of

> . . .the silly, vacant *laugh*, which is constantly observed in dementia praecox. There is no joyous humour corresponding to this laugh; indeed, some patients complain that they cannot help laughing, without feeling at all inclined to laugh.[4]

His equally influential contemporary, Eugen Bleuler, in describing schizophrenia, remarks that:

> Among the affective disturbances compulsive laughter is especially frequent; it rarely has the character of hysterical laughing fit, but that of a soulless mimic utterance behind which no feeling is noticable. . . . Sometimes the patients feel only the movements of the facile muscles ("the drawn laughter").[5]

Paradoxically, while schizophrenics may laugh, and even laugh excessively, in situations which most of us would regard as inappropriate or unhumorous, at the same time they often seem unable to enjoy appropriately humorous events or jokes. In fact, another of the hallmarks of schizophrenia is "anhedonia," a morbid inability to experience real pleasure or mirth or joy.

63

At times, schizophrenics appear too serious, as though they want to make something of grave import out of happenings or words that are intended, in the context, to be funny. I have watched acutely schizophrenic patients in the day-rooms of psychiatric wards, dolefully assembled before television sets, gazing, unsmiling and unlaughing, at the nightly dose of situation comedies. The expressions on their faces as they watch those supposedly humorous productions are serious, strained, perhaps even more so than are their expressions as they view the joyless and grim soap operas in the early afternoon.

A schizophrenic person gives the impression of someone who is straining to maintain his fragile grip on reality. In his struggle against his tendency to regress to an early level of functioning, he presumably finds funny things too threatening. Laughter and humor, involving as they do the evocation of a play mood, the temporary creation of a special context in which things are not to be taken as "real" or "serious," threaten the schizophrenic's tenuous hold on reality even more. Remember that, much earlier, we characterized humor as a kind of joint, socially sanctioned regression. Perhaps, in his turmoil, the schizophrenic fears that, were he to go along and join in the regression, he might find himself unable to return from this state.

Some jokes and humorous stories—a few theorists would say all of them—have underlying themes of sex or aggression. While the "normal" person skips lightly over these underlying themes in order to appreciate and enjoy the "point" schizophrenics tend in their interpretation of humorous material to stick very close to these themes. The schizophrenic person may feel very much threatened by these partially concealed motifs, and may have an inclination to dwell upon and elaborate the themes in a way reflective of his own inner emotional conflicts.

Of the specific sub-types of schizophrenia, it is the one called hebephrenia in which malfunctions of laughter and of the sense of humor seem to be most prominently involved. Hebephrenics are extremely regressed. They are often quite untidy, since they are unable to pay much attention to their appearance. They have a marked defect in their ability to plan things out, or to put their plans into action. Their behavior is often characterized in the textbooks as appearing "silly." Their emotional responses are typically extremely inappropriate. Hebephrenics may wear fixed, "silly'" grins, and are given to frequent, eruptive outbursts of infelicitous giggling or laughter. If one tells a hebephrenic patient a sad story, or if he hears about a tragic event, such as a death in his family, he may very well laugh or giggle. It is occasionally affirmed that hebephrenics delight in childish pranks and practical jokes, or that they enjoy costuming themselves or making themselves up.

When one asks hebephrenic patients why they are laughing, or what they are laughing at, they may have enough insight to reply that they know that their laughter is a manifestation of their illness. Or, they sometimes relate how for them, laughter provides a kind of release of tension; they don't feel quite as anxious after the laughter as they did before. So, it is as though they use their laughter as a mechanism for discharging anxiety.

Finally, it should not be forgotten that, just as inappropriate mirth is a hallmark of this illness, the reappearance of appropriate responses of mirth and joy can signal or reveal the patient's re-emergence from his psychosis. I remember very well the first schizophrenic patient I ever treated and how frustrating it was going on for so many days, and then weeks, not being able to establish genuine communication with this person. She seemed to be completely removed from the place where everyone else and I seemed to be, and her use of language was simply incomprehensible. I remember my own great joy when, at last, this woman smiled at me, not the "silly, vacant" smile of schizophrenia, but a smile of genuine human warmth and humor.

People who exhibit a paranoid personality (or paranoid psychosis, whose symptoms are even more extreme) strike others as extremely querulous, argumentative, and suspicious. Their inner worlds consist of elaborate, systematized delusions which are, on the whole, immune to logic. Attempts to reason these persons out of their delusional beliefs are not successful. These delusions are often persecutory in nature; the paranoid believes that others are out to get him, or that some sinister conspiracy is marshalling its forces against him. He thinks of his overt combativeness and hostility toward others as a natural and reasonable response to the supposed hostility of others toward him.

Paranoid individuals noticeably lack a sense of humor. They are unable to laugh at themselves or their own weaknesses; they take jokes made about them too seriously. They are likely to interpret such a jest as an overt hostile attack, as an unforgivable affront, or as representing an unbridled threat to life or well-being. Alternatively, one might say that paranoid types are unable to gain that broad perspective from which many things in the world take on a somewhat comical aspect. For the paranoid, the world is rampant with

66

sinister, secretive organizations, conspiracies and forces of a singularly serious and unfunny nature. In his tormented inner world, alas, there is very little which is deserving of a good, hearty laugh. Unfortunately, the prognosis in his case is very guarded. Although on occasion, a paranoid state can be a brief, transitory affair, or can stabilize and isolate itself from the rest of the patient's personality, the tendency is often for it to progress insidiously over the years. The patient tends to get worse and worse; from his perspective, more and more former friends appear to join the conspiracy against him until at last his inner life is a continual nightmare.

Mania is a condition which in some ways presents itself as the opposite of depression. Manic patients seem to possess an energy level which has been boosted almost miraculously. They are constantly dashing about in a great flurry of activity, chattering in an excited, happy and agitated way. So intense is this "pressure of speech," this need to verbalize the many grandiose ideas and feelings which are boiling over in their minds, that they actually become hoarse, almost losing their voices. Their mood is elevated and they are buoyant and cheerful.

It is important, for their own good, that manic patients be contained during their flights of elation. They tend to conceive extravagant schemes to save the world or to make huge bundles of money and, since their critical faculties are significantly diminished during these episodes, would try to put their unrealistic schemes into effect were they not restrained.

Marked and uninhibited high humor is a hallmark of mania. These patients are constantly cracking jokes and bubbling over with witticisms, and they love to laugh. Generally, at least initially, their humor is pleasant and joyous. However, those in the grips of mania can hardly count patience among their virtues. Accordingly, if the tiniest frustration or stumbling block thwarts them, their humor can rapidly become quite sardonic, biting, and insulting.

The high spirits and gaily funny attitude of manic patients are exceedingly contagious. For this reason, it is interesting to watch video tapes of sessions in which psychotherapists interview people with manic disorders. Once in a while it happens that, as the manic patient bounces round the room in his euphoria, the doctor himself begins to become a bit bubbly, humorous, and cheerful as if picking up the mirth through contagion.

The laughter of manic patients has its own distinctive quality. Though it is somehow appropriate, in that it fits into the context and occurs in response to jokes, etc., it sounds rapid, forced, loud, and impatient.

Hysteria is one of the most difficult of the classical mental disorders to characterize, in part due to the fact that, because of its very essence, it can present to the physician any of a bewildering array of symptoms. One typical picture is that in which a patient arrives with a list of complaints for which no organic cause or basis can be found. He or she may have an inexplicable paralysis of a limb, for instance, or an absence of some sensory function, such as seeing or hearing, or, perhaps aches and pains of a strange, shifting nature. Nonetheless, through all of this a patient may show a characteristic lack of concern (called *la belle indifference*) about these symptoms. Subsequent investigation may reveal these puzzling symptoms to be the result of emotional conflict of which the patient is not completely aware, conflict that has been repressed into the unconscious mind because the

68

emotional pain of confronting it consciously would be too much for the patient to bear.

What is called dissociation may also be a prominent feature in hysteria. In dissociation, whole aspects of a person's personality or behavior become, as it were, separated from his conscious mind and awareness, and are divorced from his wilful control. Perhaps the most widely dramatized and popularized example of this is the so-called "multiple personality" in which two or more distinct "persons" seem to manifest themselves through the same body. But there are other forms of dissociation as well. Fugue states, in which people may leave home and finally "come to" far away in unfamiliar surroundings with no recollection of how they got there, and certain dramatic cases of amnesia are both instances of dissociation.

Easily provoked, frequent, and theatrical displays of laughing and weeping have long been noted as features of hysteria. As Dr. Eugen Bleuler notes in his *Textbook of Psychiatry,* "Laughing and crying spells without any clear motivation are not rare."[6] Occasionally, there are reports of individuals who are overcome by fits of unquenchable laughter which persist for seemingly incredible periods of time. Robert Burton quotes Wolfius describing a man who

> being by chance at a sermon, saw a woman fall off from
> a form half asleep, at which object most of the com-
> pany laughed, but he for his part was so much moved,
> that for three whole days after he did nothing but laugh,
> by which means he was much weakened, and worse a
> long time following.[7]

The American physiologist Walter Cannon relates the story of a man who began laughing at 10 o'clock one morning, and was not able to stop until 4 o'clock that afternoon.

Laughing attacks of this type are likely to be labelled "hysterical laughter," and, indeed, the designation is probably apt. For, in all probability, the explanation of most of these cases, if no organic pathology is found to be associated with them, is that they are a manifestation of hysteria. Dr. Franz Alexander, one of the pioneers in the field of psychosomatic medicine, gave an interesting explanation of hysterical laughter in terms of dissociation.[5] He proposed that laughter serves to express emotion and at the same time to release emotional tension. Since, in hysterical laughter, the laugher has repressed the very emotions which the laughter would normally serve to express, the laugher has no idea, consciously, of why he is laughing. Due to this dissociation of the laughter itself from the repressed emotions, the patient does not experience the release of tension which normally takes place in laughter. Accordingly, the laughter seems uncontrollable and tends to go on for considerable lengths of time.

So, we have seen that many of the classical types of mental disorders involve defects, alterations, or peculiarities in laughter and/or the sense of humor. Still, there is much involved here which is difficult if not impossible to convey in the form of written descriptions. It is hard to produce a verbal account of the quality of schizophrenic laughter, for example. One must hear it in order to be able to empathize with such descriptions. In a way, the impression one receives when hearing the types of laughter we have discussed can be more clearly evoked by poets and literary artists than in the straightforward, literal, scientific prose of textbooks. Perhaps it is the hollow laughter of schizophrenia which is being described in a particularly haunting line by Edgar Allan Poe.

In a poem found within the text of his story "The Fall of the House of Usher," he writes of a bewitched castle, from which ". . . a hideous throng rush out forever, and laugh, but smile no more." Or, Thomas Gray might have had manic laughter in mind when he wrote of "moody madness, laughing wild."

It is not quite enough, however, to have looked at defects of mirth in the more blatant disturbances of thinking, feeling, or overt behavior that are found in the so-called mental illnesses. For, there is not a sharp dividing line, but rather a gradual shading between those behaviors and attitudes which we regard as mad and those which we regard as normal.

In this gray zone are numerous conditions which might be considered illnesses in that they cause a great deal of distress for people who are victims of them. In fact, although some might want to argue that afflictions in this category are not within the purview of medicine, the practical fact of the matter is that people sometimes come to physicians with these complaints. Hence, there is some justification for discussing such conditions within a medical context.

Three disorders falling within this category are of specific interest to us in that in various ways they exhibit defects in mirth. Two of these—shyness and boredom—are both common and widely recognized. The third, which I shall call "contrary laughter," is quite common, but has not been widely recognized by the public or in the medical literature.

Shyness is a condition which is quite difficult precisely to define, although almost everyone seems to be able to recognize certain behavior as exemplifying it. I suppose that pediatricians are consulted more often about this problem than are other medical specialists. Parents may bring their child in to the doctor for a routine examination and, in the course of the check-up, the mother or father may mention with some concern that the child is painfully shy. Psychiatrists and psychologists, too, frequently hear patients complain that they are shy. As a matter of fact, according to one report, the forthcoming edition of the manual which psychiatrists use to diagnose mental disorders will for the first time include shyness as a diagnostic category.

It is interesting to note that patients who state that they have trouble relating to others because of shyness often incidentally remark that they are afraid that others will laugh at them. They may even trace their shyness to being teased or laughed at during early life, and can sometimes relate painful childhood memories of these events.

. Obviously, people who laugh or joke a lot are not likely to be judged shy by other people, but it is most important to remember that appearances can be deceiving. Most of us would think of comedians as being outgoing, confident people, and yet in one study of this group, it was found that many of these people characterized themselves as being sensitive, shy individuals.

Both being bored and being boring are conditions which can be said, in a certain respect, to comprise a deficiency in the sense of humor. People may complain to their doctor that they feel bored all the time. Although one must, of course, be aware that such complaints can simply represent masked depression, or, what is worse, can be a forewarning of the anhedonia of incipient schizophrenia, there is no doubt that there are many people for whom boredom itself is the primary problem. A chronically bored person seems to be deficient in the ability to enjoy himself, to be amused, to have fun, to laugh.

In a period in which more and more leisure time is becoming available to an ever broader segment of the population, the problem for those who simply don't know how to have a good time is becoming worse and worse. This dilemma has become so severe that consulting firms have actually been established which do nothing but assist hard-driving, work-oriented individuals in trying to find fun things to do with their leisure time.

The boring person seems to lack a sense of humor in that he takes himself or his interests too seriously. In the end, though, the suffering here is inflicted by him upon others. He seems to be unable to amuse others or to make them laugh with him. (They may, of course, laugh *at* him, usually behind his back.)

The final group of persons in this gray area of not-quite-normal humor are those who are troubled with contrary laughter. These are people for whom laughter is the characteristic response to sad or tragic news, events or situations to which the customary or expected response is one of crying or weeping. People with contrary laughter may report, for instance, that they laugh at funerals, or upon hearing of the death of a close friend or relative, or at other sad or distressing news. They may relate that they experience the appropriate feelings of sadness or distress on such occasions; it is just that laughter, not crying, is the expressive response that comes forth. They often report that this behavior is a great source of embarrassment to them; they worry about what others who hear them might say or think.

73

The authors of one study, published in 1897, collected a considerable number of instances of this type of behavior. They observe that:

> Opposite as are our states of pleasure and pain, their expression is not so dissimilar but that in some cases of immaturity, hysteria or extreme provocation, they are confused. Cases of each of these are such as the following: A company of young people, of both sexes, from 19 to 24, were studying together when the death of an acquaintance was announced. They looked at each other for a second and then all began to laugh, and it was some time before they could become serious.
>
> F., 20. Must always laugh when she hears of a death, and has had to leave the church at a funeral because she must giggle. F., 18. On hearing of the death of a former schoolmate felt very sorry, but could not control her feelings, and laughed as heartily as she had ever done in her life. Despite her effort to be serious she had to break out into a laugh repeatedly. F., 19. Often laughs when she hears people speak of the death of their friends, not because it is funny or pleases her, but because she cannot help it.[9]

One might add to this list the case mentioned by another author of a woman who was entangled in the works of a machine and was barely saved from being maimed or killed. In response, she collapsed onto a table and laughed heartily.

Although such responses would strike most of us as being exceedingly rare, I have found quite a few people who report this problem, and I believe it to be more common than is generally recognized. It is certainly less common statistically than is the opposite phenomenon—namely, weeping at funny material, which is so common as to seem quite normal.

74

Both phenomena provide support for the claim that laughing and weeping are intimately related responses.

Since people who have contrary laughter are likely to be ashamed of it, it is important to make clear that this type of laughter, though it may be socially inappropriate, is not a manifestation of schizophrenia or other mental disorders. It is interesting to speculate that these people may literally be "laughing to keep from crying." To quote Lord Byron's words in *Don Juan*, "And if I laugh at any mortal thing/'Tis that I may not weep."

To summarize briefly: In my opinion, deviations in laughter and the sense of humor play a very profound role in mental illnesses, and the understanding of humor and laughter play a correspondingly significant role in understanding patients with mental illnesses. In 1900, Sigmund Freud published a book about dreams and their meaning in the psychological life of man. In 1905, he published a book about laughter, humor, and the comic. Since that time, his ideas about dreams have been made the focus of a technique of diagnosis and therapy for a great number of mental and emotional disorders. Suppose he had written his book on laughter first. Would psychiatry today be a very different field? One wonders. . . .

At the very beginning of this chapter I stated that the story about Democritus and Hippocrates illustrated two points, and that discussion of the second would be postponed until the end of the chapter. That point is, in short, that there is a very profound distinction between the laughter of madness and what one would call the laughing attitude toward life. We have described mad laughter above. What, then, can we say about the laughing attitude to life?

75

A few persons, perhaps a very few, can attain a perspective from which many of the foibles of mankind are viewed as a comedy being played out on a stage. These people often have incisive analytic abilities and can perceive the contradictions in the actions and words of their fellow human beings without thereby losing their love for them. They act as though, having been given a choice between getting so involved in worldly affairs as to become depressed by them, or, on the other hand, remaining detached from these events and simply enjoying them, they have unapologetically chosen the happier course. This sort of philosophical view, though rare, cannot be classified as a psychotic illness. Indeed, some might argue that this attitude should be counted as a sign of emotional health. So, it is important that one not confuse this viewpoint with mad laughter. Democritus' friends, employing rather loose criteria of mental illness, had, in their concern for him, made this mistake. Hippocrates, in his wisdom, was able to distinguish between the two.

VI

The Pathology of Laughter: Occupational and Iatrogenic Causes

Modern medicine is well aware of the importance of factors of an artificial nature in the causation of certain diseases, factors, that is, which are not so much present in nature as they are caused by man's customs and activities. Two branches of the field of medicine which are highly attuned to this are occupational medicine and the study of iatrogenic illness. *Iatrogenic* conditions are those which are caused by the doctor, as an unintended consequence of the therapeutic intervention itself. *Occupational medicine* deals with maladies to which people are subject because of hazards connected with the kind of work they do. Both of these areas of medicine bear importantly upon our topic of the pathology of laughter and humor, and we shall now consider their respective implications for this study.

77

CONTRAINDICATIONS:
WHEN NOT TO USE HUMOR

Hippocrates formulated the maxim, "Above all, do no harm," and made it the first principle of his code of medical ethics. In the contemporary medical world, this motto is assuming an ever-increasing relevance. As techniques and medications grow more sophisticated, the dangers associated with their possible misapplication grow. Almost every drug or procedure has its contraindications; that is, there are conditions in which it should *not* be used, since to do so under those circumstances would be injurious to the patient. For example, common aspirin—so beneficial to most people with pain or fever or inflammation—is contraindicated if the patient has a history of peptic ulcer disease. For, one side effect of aspirin is that it decreases the ability of the blood to clot. Hence, aspirin might cause renewed bleeding from ulcers.

Facts such as these should alert us to the possibility of the harmful misuse of humor and laughter within the medical setting. Some of the historical proponents of humor therapy whose opinions have been cited were well aware of this possibility, and tried to deal with it. Burton's enthusiastic advocacy of mirth therapy for sadness did not prevent him from recognizing that the *type* of humor to be employed in the therapy was an essential consideration, and that using the wrong type resulted in great harm. Indeed, he listed "bitter jests" as one of the causes of melancholy:

> It is an old saying, "A blow with a word strikes deeper than a blow with a sword". . . . Many men are undone by this means, moped, and so dejected, that they are never to be recovered; and of all other men living, those

78

which are actually melancholy, or inclined to it, are
most sensible and impatient of an injury of that kind;
they aggravate, and so meditate continually of it, that it
is a perpetual corrosive, not to be removed till time wear
it out.

Such scurrile jests, and sarcasms, therefore, ought
not at all to be used; especially to those that are in
misery, or anyway distressed.[1]

Burton was also careful to warn that humor therapy
could be carried too far. He pointed out that by espousing a
humorous attitude too vigorously, it is conceivable that the
physician could encourage his saddened, over-serious patient
to err in the opposite direction.

But see the mischief; many men, knowing that merry
company is the only medicine against melancholy, will
therefore neglect their business, and in another extreme,
spend all their days among good fellows in a tavern or
an ale-house, and know not otherwise how to bestow
their time but in drinking; like so many frogs in a
puddle.[2]

More generally than even Burton allowed, it is certainly
true that for some persons, a humorous approach would
definitely be inadvisable. Three distinct groups of patients
who fall into this category should be noted here: First, those is
for whom laughter and joy have become guilt-provoking and
threatening states; second, those who have some constitu-
tional pecularity in which joy or elation may provoke unpleasant physical symptoms; and third, those who have some
disease or injury for which laughter has adverse effects.

As to the first group: It is well recognized that some
persons are actually fearful of joy, elation, pleasure and other
usually positive emotional states. In many of these people,

being joyful or experiencing pleasure cause them to have feelings of guilt, shame or unworthiness. This generally is due to unresolved emotional conflicts, usually stemming from much earlier periods of their lives, and of which they may not even be consciously aware. A specific sub-group of these persons consists of those who despise humor and laughter. These dour souls studiously and conscientiously avoid hearty laughter and mirth, often rationalizing their behavior by appealing to puritanical or ascetic standards of conduct, or "gentlemanly" codes of etiquette. Meredith characterized such people quite well.

> We have in this world men whom [one might] call "agelasts," that is to say, non-laughers. . . . The old gray boulder-stone, that has finished its peregrination from the rock to the valley, is as easily to be set rolling up again as these men laughing. No collision of circumstances in our mortal career strikes a light for them. It is but one step from being agelastic to misogelastic, and . . . the laughter-hating person soon learns to dignify his dislike as an objection in morality.[3]

Lord Chesterfield exemplified Meredith's "misogelastic" or laughter-hating character quite well. In a letter to his son dated October 19, 1748, he wrote:

> Loud Laughter is the mirth of the mob, who are only pleased with silly things; for true Wit or good Sense never excited a laugh since the creation of the world. A man of parts and fashion is therefore only seen to smile, but never heard to laugh.[5]

This nobleman's objection to mirth originates in his idea of what it is to be a gentleman. As an example of one whose objection stems from principles of religious asceticism one can hardly do better than to cite the words of Saint John

Chrysostom, Archbishop of Constantinople, and early
Church father who lived from 345 to 407 A.D.:

> . . . to laugh, to speak jocosely, does not seem an ac-
> knowledged sin, but it leads to acknowledged sin. Thus
> laughter often gives birth to foul discourse, and foul
> discourse to actions still more foul. Often from words
> and laughter proceed railing and insult; and from
> railing, and insult, blows and wounds; and from blows
> and wounds, slaughter and murder. If, then, thou
> wouldst take good counsel for thyself, avoid not merely
> foul words, and foul deeds, or blows, and wounds, and
> murders, but unseasonable laughter, itself.[5]

At a later point in the same work, he continues his attack
on hilarity by sounding an even more ominous warning:

> Suppose some persons laugh. Do thou on the other hand
> weep for their transgressions. Many also once laughed at
> Noah whilst he was preparing the ark; but when the
> flood came, he laughed at them; or rather, the just man
> never laughed at them at all, but wept and bewailed.
> When therefore thou seest persons laughing, reflect that
> those teeth, that grin now, will one day have to sustain
> that most dreadful wailing and gnashing, and that they
> will remember this same laugh on That Day whilst they
> are grinding and gnashing. Then thou too shalt re-
> member this laugh.[6]

One ruler of old should surely be added to our list of
non-laughers. Dr. Doran in *The History of Court Fools* tells his
story:

> . . . it was not every King . . . who cared to be moved to
> laughter by the exhibitions of comic minstrels or jocu-
> lators. Some princes have indeed accounted laughter
> thus raised, as beneath the dignity of men of their rank.
> Thus Philip, son of the Christian Emperor Philip the

81

Arabian, rebuked his own sire openly, for laughing at the jokes and sports of hired jesters who were doing their best to amuse the sovereign and an august body of spectators. The younger Philip read the elder Philip a severe lecture on his unseeming conduct, which seems to me to have been a greater offence against propriety, than his father's merriment. The son's contemporaries gave him the name of Philip Agelastos; and he has come down to us as Philip the Laughless.[7]

Related, perhaps, to the above attitudes, but less extreme, is the behavior of those unfortunate souls who seem forever "slow" to get the point of the jest. No doubt we all know someone who always seems to be the last in the group to laugh, who stands there with a baffled, groping, and somewhat helpless expression on his face, meekly and hesitantly pleading for an explanation of the joke, even while everyone around him is collapsing in merriment.

Another group of laughter-resistant individuals consists of those who are forever misunderstanding humor by taking remarks made in jest as though they were intended to be serious. This group is of special interest to me, because I have a very whimsical sense of humor which extremely serious types occasionally misconstrue. It is intriguing to ask what makes some prone to misinterpret humor, and it is a problem which has not been investigated with much thoroughness. We have seen in Chapter V that this can occur in paranoid states, but it can also occur in the absence of psychopathology. Interestingly, the results of some psychological studies suggest that there is a correlation between this kind of misunderstanding of humor, on the one hand, and prejudice on the other.

Whatever the causes of laughter-resistance, it is fairly obvious that in cases like the above, in which resistance to mirth is so extreme, a humorous approach may well be threatening to a patient and can have the effect of increasing his distress. Before humor can be used effectively, the unconscious conflicts which hamper the person's ability to enjoy himself have to be identified, brought to his consciousness, and removed.

A second broad group of patients for whom humor therapy might well be contraindicated are those who experience unpleasant physical symptoms during states of elation and joy, including laughter. Dr. Ian Stevenson has collected a total of twenty-one instances of this phenomenon, which he has reported in two articles in medical journals.[8] In these cases, various distressing symptoms, including urinary urgency, cardiac palpitations or arrhythmias, gastro-intestinal upsets, and skin eruptions were reported to occur during moods of joyfulness or elation. There was no evidence, in these instances, that the patient's annoying symptoms resulted from unconscious conflicts or guilt feelings concerning pleasure or joy.

Dr. Stevenson offers an interesting hypothesis to explain these unusual observations. Perhaps, he suggests, a habituation mechanism is involved. All of these patients had noted the same distressing symptoms during negative emotional states, such as anxiety or despair. He believes it is possible that, by reacting to negative emotional states with these symptoms, the nervous system may gradually become so accustomed to producing them that it creates a response-pattern which may occur during any sort of arousal, even pleasurable arousal.

Dr. Stevenson's findings have, as he points out, much practical value. People who do not consciously feel unhappy are for that reason more likely to resist their physician's attempts to explain their physical symptoms in psychosomatic terms. They are all the more likely to do so if they are happy or elated when the symptoms occur. So, an awareness that happy feelings as well as anxious feelings can trigger distressing physical symptoms is important for physicians.

Our third group of patients for whom laughter should be dispensed with caution consists of those who have diseases or medical conditions in which laughter has potentially adverse effects. Prominent among these conditions is narcolepsy, a bizarre disorder of sleep. People with narcolepsy have frequent attacks, during the daytime, of an irresistable need to sleep. They may doze off sitting upright in a chair, in the middle of a conversation with friends, or even when engaged in an activity such as driving a car.

They also suffer from sleep paralysis; they awaken from sleep feeling alert and aware but are completely unable to move the muscles of their body. They must struggle in this frightening predicament until the spell is broken, for instance, by moving a single joint or a finger, or when someone else in the room touches them. They may have hypnagogic hallucinations—strange, surrealistic images, often of a frightening character—which flash before their minds as they drift off to sleep.

A significant proportion of persons with narcolepsy also have cataplexy. Cataplexy is a condition in which the occurrence of intense emotional states results in a sudden, dramatic loss of muscle tone, so that the person collapses and falls to the floor, paralyzed. Throughout the attack, however, he remains acutely alert and aware of what is going on, finding his inability to move extremely unpleasant and alarming.

Laughter is commonly found to bring about a cataplectic collapse in these persons. It is interesting to note that they will sometimes learn to avoid mirth-provoking people or situations. I once had a narcoleptic patient who was so frustrated by her cataplexy that she said she never told jokes herself and had adopted the practice of "turning my mind off" when others began telling them. She was constantly fearful that if she started laughing heartily she might collapse before her friends, alarming them and embarrassing herself.

The cause of narcolepsy is unknown. Fortunately, however, the sleep attacks can be controlled to a degree by administering stimulants, such as tea, coffee, and the drug methylphenidate.

Another condition which might be mentioned here is Tietze's syndrome. This is an inflammation and swelling involving one or more rather circumscribed areas of the cartilages which join the ribs to the sternum or breastbone in the chest. No one knows what causes it, but it is manifested as a sharp pain in the chest which becomes more severe when the person is coughing or breathing deeply, as in hearty laughter. People who get Tietze's syndrome often become alarmed and think that they have heart disease. The treatment is to reassure them that the condition is not serious. Aspirin helps control the inflammation and pain, but in most cases spontaneous resolution takes place within a few weeks, even without treatment. Obviously, vigorous mirth should be avoided in these patients as it should be immediately following abdominal surgery: It would hurt too much.

There are a few other, more general pitfalls of the

therapeutic use of humor and laughter which should not go unmentioned. Above all, it should not be pretended that mirth is a panacea, a specific cure for all of mankind's ills. Humor must be used very cautiously, for it can be used as a psychological defense mechanism, by both physician and patient. No one would want to use humor in such a way as to encourage a patient to laugh off a serious illness and thereby to refrain from seeking medical attention for it.

Furthermore—and this is very important—it is clear that humor is not a substitute for honesty. Jokes and lies, though both may be in some sense "untrue" or "fictional," are not the same thing. Obviously, a physician should not allow his enthusiasm for keeping his patient's spirits high to shade over into deceit, to avoid facing the truth, for example, about a grave condition. That this could occur is not unthinkable. Thus, de Mondeville, just after he proposes that the surgeon keep his patient happy by providing jokes and music, goes on to recommend that the same end might also be furthered "by forged letters describing the death of his enemies, or by telling him that he has been elected to a bishopric, if a churchman."[9]

It is almost unbelievable to us today that this idea was seriously proposed by a respectable medieval medical authority. Our sense of shock should stand as a potent reminder that humor has a positive role to play in treatment, and not the purely negative one of avoiding frankness and forthrightness in the doctor-patient relationship.

One final note relates specifically to clowning in the hospital setting. Having seen an experienced professional clown in action in a pediatrics ward, I can see quite clearly the dangers that could lie in amateurs attempting to do the same thing. An experienced clown has learned to maintain exactly the correct amount of space between himself and the children he entertains; he steps back automatically, just the right distance, should a child become fearful. A skilled clown's magic show succeeds apparently without effort because of long years of practice. A beginner's well-intentioned efforts could very well frighten children; he might inadvertently injure them with his illusionist tricks. In short, I am convinced that in professional clowns we have a very valuable, and largely untapped, medical resource. The brotherhood of clowns is very ancient indeed. We ought to acknowledge the fact that theirs is a laboriously learned skill by making sure that only seasoned practitioners of the art perform for ill patients.

Finally, some might protest that the very concept of humor therapy is impossible in that therapy is not fun; it is work! This objection, however, is a purely rhetorical one, because humor is not the opposite of work. For, if it were, then there could be no such thing as a professional comedian. This leads us naturally into our next topic.

SICK COMICS:
OCCUPATIONAL HAZARDS OF FUNNY MEN

The story is told that sometime in the last century a prominent European physician was examining an elderly man. After checking him over thoroughly and listening to his many vague complaints, the physician could find nothing physically wrong which would account for this patient's symptoms. We might imagine that it occurred to the doctor, just as it might to one of his latter-day colleagues that his patient's physical complaints were in all probability serving as a mask for deep-seated emotional stress and depression. Suddenly, an inspired idea came to him. It happened that Joseph Grimaldi, perhaps the greatest clown of all times, was in town for a performance that very evening. The physician shrugged his shoulders about his inability to arrive at a diagnosis and suggested to the patient, "Why don't you go to see Grimaldi tonight?" A distressed and disappointed expression suddenly played across the old man's face, and he exclaimed, "Oh, but you don't understand. I *am* Grimaldi!"

This story, often told as though true, may be apocryphal. Regardless of its literal truth or falsity, this anecdote illustrates a belief so widespread that is has almost become an item of folk wisdom—the belief that funny people are basically sad at heart.

Various bits of what may be loosely termed "evidence" are customarily adduced to support this idea. Abraham Lincoln is often given as an example of an extremely humorous person who had a severely depressive and sad side as well. Or, one might allude to the documentable background of struggle and deprivation present in the early lives of many persons who have later enjoyed success as comedians. As a matter of fact, some might go so far as to say that, in some instances, the very sadness of a clown or comedian—or at least of the character he portrays—is an essential part of what makes him funny to us.

Furthermore, some of the professional jargon of comedians could be brought up in support of this notion. We all know that instead of saying "good luck" to an actor in a play, one is supposed to say, "Break a leg." Paradoxically, in that situation it is regarded as "bad luck" to say, "good luck."

What is not so widely known is that a similar custom is in force among comedians, one with an interesting twist. For, if a comedian is about to perform, his fellows are enjoined to say, not "good luck," but, rather "slit a wrist."

This and other quirks of the language of professional funny men could be deemed insignificant. On the other hand, they could be interpreted as betraying deep-seated masochistic tendencies. The masochistic person is seeking pain, or even his own destruction, as a way of punishing himself for real or imagined crimes or sins he feels he has committed. Much of his behavior is motivated by an urge or desire—albeit usually unconscious—to harm himself, or at least to get others to hurt him, by putting himself into situations in which this will happen. Naturally, severe depression and feelings of worthlessness are very common concomitants of masochistic dispositions.

So, if the above rankly speculative analysis approximates the reality of the situation, then the proverbial sadness of humorists could be seen as the consequence of unconscious tendencies toward self-harm. It is important, however, to emphasize that this is speculative, since, as far as I have been able to discover, there has been little systematic investigation of the psychological makeup of humorous people. Comedians, clowns, and comic writers may, of course, suffer from depression, but then, so may anyone. The dramatic contrast, which one grasps with such immediacy, between sadness and laughter, may predispose us all to pay more attention to depression when it occurs in a funny person.

Nonetheless, the common notion that clowns are sad serves as a pointed reminder to us of something which might otherwise be ignored. We are going through a period in which occupational medicine is increasing in importance. Almost weekly, we are learning of new ways in which the products and processes of industry can harm us, the environment, and—often most directly—the employees of industry. More generally, almost every occupation presents its own hazard to the health and well-being of those in it. As we shall see, people who earn their living by making others laugh are no exception.

There are a number of medical disorders or conditions to which clowns are especially vulnerable. One would immediately think of certain kinds of injuries: Those they might receive from objects thrown at clowns by unruly audiences, or those from falls which might occur in the acrobatic portions of their acts. There are other hazards, though, which are not so immediately obvious.

Clowns frequently experience an increasing dimunition of the acuity of their hearing as the season progresses. The cause for this lies in the traditional method for applying clown make-up. They store their supply of powder in a sock, and apply it by vigorously beating the sock. As the powder comes through the fabric, it forms a billowing cloud around the clown's head and chest, and some of it adheres to the compound which has already been applied to his face. An undesirable consequence of this is that some of the floating powder drifts into the ear canal. There, over a period of time, it combines with the ear wax to form a dense, hard mass which gradually decreases the clown's ability to hear. One of my clown friends described to me how his hearing seems to worsen as the season goes on. Then, sometime after the season is over, he hears a loud pop as the ear finally clears itself of this plug, and he can suddenly hear well again.

There is another complication of the use of make-up

which often plagues clowns. The compounds used in the make-up cannot be kept sterile. They may become infected with microorganisms. Sometimes, especially during a period of frequent engagements in which the make-up has had to be worn for a long time, this may result in an annoying and potentially serious eye infection.

Surprisingly, chimpanzee bites are another occupational hazard of clowning. For some reason, which even life-long circus workers are hard-pressed to explain, chimps hate clowns and will viciously attack them if given the opportunity. For this reason, circus ring managers take a great deal of care about the relative placement of chimps and clowns. It has happened that clowns have been severely bitten and scratched by enraged chimpanzees.

Those whose job it is to write humorous material, whether for performance by themselves or by others, are subject to an interesting psychological problem. In Chapter I, it was mentioned that the phrase "to have a good sense of humor" sometimes is used to designate the creative talent some have of devising new jokes and funny stories. This process apparently is subject to its own inherent dysfunctions, and, hence, comic writers are vulnerable to the same so-called "creative blocks" as are other artists.

Very little is known about the mental processes involved in creativity. Much of the creative process seems to take place at levels of the mind which are not easily accessible to conscious awareness. Consequently, even extremely creative persons, by and large, do not seem consciously to understand the process very well. They often have great difficulty when trying to explain clearly the steps which go on in their minds as their work is being produced.

One thing which can be said with some confidence

about creative blocks is that they often come about because the creative person is trying too hard to exert conscious control over the process. In effect, by trying consciously to force oneself to create something, one inhibits the unconscious factors which must be allowed some expression in order for the creative work to be done. Some persons whose work involves creating relate that at the times when they have to force it, their work seems poorest. Their best work, they say, comes during periods when it flows from them with a minimum of self-conscious direction.

Because of our lack of knowledge concerning creativity, no generally accepted treatment for "creative blocks" is available. In the absence of any reliable remedy from professionals, creative people who have this trouble generally develop their own strategies for dealing with it. A comedian who is going through a "dry period" in production of new material may employ techniques for getting the flow started again. He may go to a favorite spot, sit down in a certain chair, tidy up the room he is in, sharpen his pencils, or perform some other favored ritual.

Another occupation-related disorder is one which pertains primarily to stand-up comedians, people who entertain by performing comedy before live audiences. This condition—called "flop sweat" in the parlance of those who are potentially subject to it—is a kind of anxiety attack brought on by what comedians term "dying." In their vocabulary, "dying" is what happens when one stands up before an audience trying to be funny and no one laughs.

The following excerpt from a dialogue-interview between a comedian and myself, illustrates clearly the dramatic nature of this condition.

Comedian: You're scared to death when you realize it is happening. The audience sometimes is very, very cruel. They will just watch you die, because there is pleasure in it. But when about the fourth or fifth line that you know should have got a good laugh hasn't, you get a fear. It is like the whole world has turned on you and it scares you to death. And you don't know why but you are going to finish that bit. It is like you must finish. I've never seen anybody stop. I've never seen anybody say, "Okay, I've got to stop right here." For some stupid reason you go straight through. You're standing there and you can't step down from your own punishment.

R.M.: What about remedies for it? If that happens to you, what do you do?

Comedian: You have to know, first of all that it is their fault. You can't think it is your fault. So, I generally go some place and find an audience and work for them and make them laugh to make sure I still have the ability to do so. . . . And when it does happen to you, it is the worst feeling in the world. The silence is screaming. You know that there are some people who are feeling sorry for you, yet they won't give you a laugh.

R.M.: Does your heart beat fast?

Comedian: No, as a matter of fact, I get the feeling that it is slowing down . . . to the point where I'm going to die.

The words of this comedian clearly convey the depth of the anguish a performer may feel when he is rejected in a heartless fashion by his audience. This description points up some findings of modern psychosomatic medicine which placed renewed emphasis upon the importance of the will to live in maintaining physical health. The possibility of psy-

93

chogenic death—that is, death due to emotional causes such as grief, social rejection, "giving up," in short, loss of the will to live—has been discussed in recent medical literature. It is not too surprising to learn that in at least one recorded instance, a comedian's figurative "dying" resulted in a literal one.

In the early 1700's the French actor Hamoche portrayed the clown Pierrot at the Fair of Saint-Laurent. So resounding was his triumph in the role that he aspired to greater glory and went away to join a more reknowned company of comic actors and entertainers. When he was rebuffed by this group, he returned to the site of his original success, expecting to stage a comeback. The management of the Fair tried to put together an elaborate welcome-home; the spectators, however, had other ideas.

> The forain audience, by no means flattered at being looked upon as a last resource, hissed Hamoche by way of teaching him a lesson. This punishment so wounded the poor Pierrot that he withdrew from the theatre and died of grief.[10]

Finally, and regrettably, one must not neglect to mention among the occupational hazards of comedians, occasional banishment, harassment, persecution, and even execution or assassination, if the comedian's jests offend humorless authorities. To give only one example of many which are available: Satire was once so feared among the Arabs as an agency of magical potency that it is alleged that on two occasions Muhammed himself had satirists executed. The peril a humorist may face is especially great when the despot he offends is one of Meredith's "misogelastic" or laughter-hating characters. The African Kaffir chief Chaka would not tolerate laughter

> . . . at his horridly solemn court. On one occasion, however, and in full council, a merry fellow gave utterance to a frolicsome thought which he could not repress. It succeeded admirably—gloomy king and grave counsellors were thrown into the most convulsive hilarity. When they had all recovered, the chief, pointing towards the jester, showed his grateful sense of a rare delight, by exclaiming, "Take the dog out, and kill him; he has made me laugh![11]

So, we have seen that although humor sometimes seems healthy and therapeutic, there are many situations in which it is pathological and potentially harmful. Before looking at some suggestions for how this apparent dilemma can be resolved, we need to see one more piece of the puzzle.

VII

Society and Healing Humor

As we saw in the first chapter, humor and laughter have very important social aspects. Subsequently, we have described numerous disorders of the sense of humor involving both physiological and mental functioning of the individual. Taken together, these considerations suggest a further question: Can there be disorders or disturbances of mirth which pertain specifically to the social dimensions of life?

Chief among the modes of laughter-making which have been perverted to unfortunate social ends is ridicule. Ridicule in our own society has been institutionalized in certain forms which are probably on the whole rather harmless. These include the "roast," a ceremonial occasion upon which the victim's friends gather together in his presence in order systematically to insult and poke fun at him. The guilt which would otherwise be mobilized in the consciences of the roasters by such thinly-veiled expressions of hostility is mollified by two clever devices. First, the victim's own supposedly "voluntary" complicity is secured. It is incumbent upon him to be a "good sport," to realize that his friends are "only joking," and to use the occasion to demonstrate that he can

96

"take a joke." Secondly, the proceeds from the ritual itself are often used to support some worthy charitable cause.

Another example of a socially permitted display of humorous abuse is found in a particular comic style. Many professional comedians are identified in the public mind with the use of jesting insults. These figures have been granted a license to belittle others in a funny way, and a social convention has been established to the effect that no offense is to be taken by their targets.

Some may want to argue that "roasts" and insult humorists pose no real threat to individual well-being or to the social fabric. It might be said that they represent legitimate ways of discharging aggressive tendencies; certainly they are more desirable than is overt violence. Nonetheless, ridicule can be taken to extremes, and may have unforeseen and unfortunate consequences.

A whole society may conceivably have a cruel, sadistic sense of humor. One is struck by how ancient writers record, without registering even a faint note of protest, that in their societies people with deformities are regarded as fit objects of derisive laughter. Thus, the Roman orator, thinker and statesman, Cicero, remarks,

> Those subjects are most readily jested upon which are neither provocative of violent aversion, nor of extreme compassion. All matter for ridicule is therefore found to lie in such defects as are to be observed in the characters of men not in universal esteem, nor in calamitous circumstances, and who do not appear deserving to be dragged to punishment for their crimes; such topics nicely managed create laughter. . . . In deformity also, and bodily defects, are found fair enough matter for ridicule.[1]

Cicero is apparently not theorizing but is rather describing actual Roman practice. To give only one example, people with deforming and crippling handicaps were sometimes forced to fight gladiatorial combats in the arena at Rome, provoking hilarious mirth among the spectators. Nor were the Romans the only culprits. In a number of societies over the centuries, laughter at the deformed and the insane has been accepted as the norm.

The presence within a society of attitudes and practices of this type has immediate and profound implications for health care. For ridicule and derisive laughter may play an adverse role in the psychological development of children with deformities and can disturb their adaptation to the handicapping illness or condition. Sometimes scars are left which can be erased only with great difficulty in later life.

René Descartes long ago commented on the devastating effects of ridicule on deformed individuals.

> Derision or scorn is a sort of joy mingled with hatred, which proceeds from our perceiving some small evil in a person whom we consider to be deserving of it. . . .
>
> And we notice that people with very obvious defects such as those who are lame, blind of an eye, hunched-backed, or who have received some public insult, are specially given to mockery; for, desiring to see all others held in as low estimation as themselves, they are truly rejoiced at the evils which befall them, and they hold them deserving of these.[2]

In a similar vein, a more recent author, J. C. Gregory, has claimed,

> Since men suit their conduct to their treatment, habitual ridicule breeds temper in the ridiculed, and the dwarf of tradition was bitter because he was an object of

98

merriment. . . . Human mirth has always been easily
aroused by the spectacle of physical infirmities.[3]

The psychological impact of ridicule on the individual
personality is perhaps not so uniform as the words of
Descartes and Gregory might suggest. There seems to be
something indominatable about some people; their spirits
soar even in adversity. Some of the towering figures of history
have turned early experiences of being tormented, teased,
and ridiculed about their defects or deformities to their own
advantage and to the advantage of us all.

Occasional favorable outcomes, however, can never
excuse the practice. By tolerating laughter at deformities a
society creates a "false alien"; that is, a myth to the effect that
some human beings, because of purely structural differences,
are inwardly and morally different from their fellows. The
harmful consequences of this myth—both in terms of the
suffering of deformed persons and in terms of the ignorance
and insensitivity it confers upon those who are thereby
permitted to laugh—can hardly be underestimated. We are
indeed fortunate that, although each generation must be
educated anew, the overall trend is for this practice to die out
among us. Gregory was correct, I believe, in calling such a
direction

> An index of the humanization of laughter. . . . The
> growth of the sympathetic spirit has affected laugh-
> ter. . . . The disappearance of physical infirmity as
> recognized object of mirth intimates a wider spread and
> a deeper planting of the spirit of sympathy.[4]

Just as laughter at the different can retard understanding, laughter at the new can retard progress. Historically,
countless striking innovations have been greeted with ridi-

cule. The new is frightening and threatening so it is rejected. Ridicule is one of society's ways of preserving the *status quo*. The mere fact that an idea is new, or that it is laughed at when it is introduced, obviously is no guarantee that ultimately it will prove valid or useful. Nonetheless, the practice of laughing at what is novel has demonstrably held back the application of some of the most significant discoveries of mankind. The concepts of the telephone, and subsequently of wireless transmission of messages, the phonograph, manned flight, space travel were all at first received with self-complacent mirth.

The practice of laughing at new ideas has at times had unfavorable consequences for the public health, as well. Numerous new departures in the field of medicine which later proved pivotal were initially scorned. The technique of vaccination against infectious diseases may have been the most significant medical discovery of all time; yet, smallpox vaccination was mocked in ludicrous cartoons for some time after it was introduced. One of the pioneers in the use of anesthetic gas during surgical procedures was so ridiculed following an unsuccessful public demonstration of his technique that he became emotionally unstable and killed himself.

Ridicule is not the only type of humor which is capable of bringing about troublesome social ramifications. Concurrent with the rash of airline hijackings which took place in the United States during the 1960's and 1970's was an epidemic of jokes about hijackings among passengers. Travelers who made jokes in an entirely humorous mood suddenly found themselves in jail. This problem actually necessitated legislative measures. Airport personnel are now required by law to take seriously all statements—including those made in jest—about hijacking, bombs, and concealed weapons on board aircraft.

One might even be able to make a case for including silly or funny fads as social disturbances of the sense of humor. Fads obviously have a social nature, and while some fads are not funny, others definitely are. Everyone has within him some propensity for regression to earlier levels of development. The occurrence of certain fads depends upon these propensities being simultaneously activated in a sizable group of people. Pictures taken at humorous fad "happenings" such as telephone booth stuffings, mud baths, dance marathons, streaking bouts, and so on, often reveal bright, mirthful, smiling and laughing faces among participants and spectators alike. A festival atmosphere and a general mood of hilarity prevail. There seems to be, as it were, an epidemic of fun. There is a generalized shift in the socially established standards of what is thought to be funny or laughable.

Yet another such phenomenon is the laughing epidemic, a manifestation of group psychopathology which is well-documented in the medical literature. In 1962, in what is now Tanzania, over one thousand people were afflicted by a peculiar illness in which they were seized by uncontrollable laughter, lasting for as long as several hours.[5] The first persons known to be affected were adolescents in a mission boarding school for girls. As the laughing spread from student to student over the weeks, the illness reached such proportions that the school had to be closed and the young women were sent home. As they returned to their villages, the laughing epidemic traveled with them. The sickness had a peculiar distribution in the population: The majority of those with the

symptoms were teen-aged boys and girls, while more liter-
ate and educated members of the community were oddly
immune. Altogether, the routine social order of the region
was disturbed for a period of six months.

When physicians were called in to investigate, thorough
physical examinations and laboratory tests repeatedly failed
to reveal any organic basis for the symptoms. It was finally
concluded that the illness was an outbreak of mass or group
hysteria. The laughing epidemic appeared again in 1977,
among young women in a school. At that time, Tanzanian
officials could only console themselves with the reflection
that, although the "laughing sickness" was exceedingly difficult to deal with, the only serious feature of it was that it
disrupted classes.

To say that there can be socially condoned misuses or
disturbances of laughter and humor, however, is only half the
story. Because it has a certain social power, mirth can be
socially destructive. But that power can be employed to
benefit as well.

Many societies have tacitly acknowledged the value of
periodic mirth as a form of release from the tensions created
by social restraints. Holidays and festivals during which
routine prohibitions are relaxed, and laughter at the normally sancrosanct is encouraged, allow for the harmless
expression of hostilities and normally restrained instincts. In
some American Indian tribes, this periodic release of inhibitions was presided over by the tribal clown. This office was
regarded with profound respect, and by long-standing tradition the person filling it was accorded great veneration. Even
today we have April Fool's Day, a holiday devoted especially
to laughter and to the practical joke.

Examples of socially beneficial uses of humor could be

multiplied. The humor of the Czechoslovakian people has been cited as an important factor in their maintenance of social solidarity, as well as of individual dignity and self-respect, during the occupation of their country by the Nazis in World War II. And from time to time, one hears stories of comedians preventing panic by entertaining others in crisis situations. For example, some years ago, newspapers reported that a famous American humorist had kept spirits high and hopeful by entertaining his fellow passengers when their aircraft developed serious mechanical difficulties.

Indeed, many theorists have ascribed to comedy itself a socially therapeutic function. The most thoroughgoing proponent of this viewpoint in recent history was the French philosopher Henri Bergson. He believed that the very existence of a social order depends upon its members maintaining, through their attitudes and behavior, a vital, flexible attitude toward life. Bergson thought that ultimately what makes us laugh are situations in which someone has become inflexible to the point of losing his social elasticity. A machine-like rigidity has taken the place of a vital response to life. Laughter, as institutionalized in the work of comic dramatists or writers, has as its social function the directing of our attention to rigid behavior in ourselves and others, and hopefully the correcting of this behavior before it becomes harmful.

In response to many such examples of socially beneficial uses of humor, there have been specific proposals for more deliberate use of humor to alleviate social problems. There is even headquartered in Paris a Society for Humor in International Relations, dedicated to the promotion of mirth as a means of easing international tensions and of bringing about closer understanding among nations.

It has even been argued that humor might have a place

in the arsenal of authorities charged with riot and mob control.[6] One analyst has pointed out that the only role of the police in civil disturbances is that of maintaining order, and that, theoretically, their position is a neutral one with respect to any social issues involved. He has suggested that humor be explored as a means of averting violence during such confrontations. He listed several occasions when this had been done, including once in West Berlin during a student demonstration against the war in Vietnam. The German police, concerned because a similar demonstration not long before had erupted into violence resulting in death and injury, resolved to try humor this time. An officer who also taught psychology and who had some skill as an entertainer was chosen to be the master of ceremonies. Through the use of appropriate humor, music, and banter, he succeeded in evoking a carnival mood and forestalling violence.

In Britain, a group of behavioral scientists carried out an elaborate experiment designed to help them determine whether or not mirth promotes social harmony.[7] They planned and constructed, in a university building, what they termed a "humor environment." They equipped the area with assorted fun machinery that visitors could play with, piped in amusing sound effects, and prominently displayed printed cartoons and jokes. Clothing and masks were left in a big trunk so that people wandering in could dress themselves up, and silly toys were left lying round to be played with. Outlets for the creative expression of humor were provided, too; those coming in were invited to contribute their own captions to some of the pictures in the room.

Subjects entering the environment were encouraged to do whatever they liked. They were constantly observed while in the area by one of the scientists, who was watching from a hidden location. A hidden television camera recorded the proceedings, too. A standard psychological test which measures mood was administered to each subject, both before and after entering the area.

Results revealed that a visit to the environment was, on the whole, quite effective in elevating the spirits of the subjects. Reflecting on the significance of their findings, the researchers concluded that there is some possibility that similar "humor environments" might be of social value to communities.

In the contemporary world, we seem to be experiencing a progressive breakdown of the true sense of community, including shared ideas and aspirations. One participant at a scientific conference on humor suggested that the creation of neighborhood "laughter centers"—buildings designed to promote communally shared mirth—might be an effective means of bringing us together once again.[8]

These facts and findings raise the possiblity that, ultimately, no society is truly sound and well-ordered unless it is able to laugh at itself. If defensible, this principle is remarkably congruent with what our findings have indicated about the physical and emotional health of the individual.

Let us now recapitulate for a bit. We began with a number of observations about the nature of laughter and humor and about their physiological, emotional, and social dimensions. We next proceeded to present a series of cases suggesting that laughter and humor are healthy and therapeutic. These were shown to be supported both by folk wisdom and by a long tradition of scholarly writing. We then discussed how mirth can often be a sign, not of health, but of physical illness or emotional disturbance, and pointed out some situations in which laughter might be detrimental, rather than helpful, in the healing context. Finally, we saw how humor and laughter also have social dimensions and consequences, both undesirable and desirable, harmful and beneficial, disruptive and unifying.

So, we are in a quandary: If humor and laughter have both bad and good effects, then how is the physician to know exactly when to use them? Is there any way, other than by common sense or intuition, of distinguishing healthy laughter from unhealthy, humor that is harmful from humor that is therapeutic? In what follows, we will try to bring these observations together in a way which may help to do that. We will try, in short, to offer a preliminary explanation of the healing power of humor.

VIII

Why Humor Works

In diagnosing the ills of the medical theories and practices of his day, Socrates noted "As it is not proper to cure the eyes without the head, nor the head without the body, so neither is it proper to cure the body without the soul."

In modern times, much of this kind of sentiment has provided impetus to the study of psychosomatic medicine. Increasingly, it has become clear that mental and emotional states can give rise to organic conditions, and, conversely, that given organic diseases can affect the mind or emotions in specifiable and predictable ways. The insight that the interplay between mental and physical factors is essential to the causation of disease is the basis of psychosomatic medicine.

Regrettably, however, the term "psychosomatic" has taken on certain misleading associations. When patients are told that their illness is psychosomatic they often feel insulted, and think that they are being told that their symptoms are merely imaginary. This is an unfortunate misinterpretation, for it is a medical assumption that emotional states can produce very real, indeed measurable, changes in the structure and function of the body.

More broadly, it might be suggested that the term "psychosomatic" focuses attention on each person as an individual mind-body unit, neglecting the importance of health factors having their origin in the social aspects of life. "Healing" in its original sense meant "making whole." Hopefully, we are developing toward a broader concept of medicine in which we pay attention not only to the body and to the mind, but also to the functioning of the person within his social context, and, ultimately, within the natural environment as well.

The use of humor and laughter as therapy falls within the context of such a broader approach to medicine. As we have already seen, laughter and humor have not only physiological and psychological aspects but pervasive social ones as well. Laughter and humor integrate the physiological, the psychological, and the social events and processes that shape each person as do few other phenomena. This fact gives us an overall perspective from which to view many findings about mirth and its relationship to health and to illness.

The question which now confronts us is this: Why are humor and laughter sometimes therapeutic, and what most generally distinguishes healthy uses of mirth from unhealthy ones? An approach to the second part of this question might be made by considering the relation to laughter of a term which I have used in earlier chapters. In the discussion of the occurrence of mirth in disease and madness, certain types of laughter were characterized time and time again as "inappropriate." But, someone might object, what are the standards for deciding what is appropriate and inappropriate laughter, and who gets to decide?

It is not enough to say that certain types of laughter or humor are inappropriate because they result from lesions in the brain. The fact that the disorders of mirth found in patients with such diseases as pseudobulbar palsy, kuru, epilepsy, and the pre-senile dementias are associated with identifiable changes or lesions in the brain is obviously important. However, people recognized that there is something wrong about the laughter of the victims of these diseases long before science discovered and pinpointed the brain lesions found in the diseases. Similarly, today one can recognize that there is something wrong or inappropriate about the mirth of patients with hysteria, schizophrenia, or mania, even though at present science is not aware of any brain lesions or changes associated with these conditions.

The explanation for why certain humor and laughter is called "inappropriate" lies on a different and more inclusive level. Ultimately, in order to be interpreted as a healthy response, mirth must occur within the context of a network of mutually understanding, loving, and supporting human relationships. It is precisely its failure to fit into this network of mutually understanding, loving, and supportive human relationships which makes us call some humor and laughter pathological. Thus, the laughter of some epileptics is pathological in part because it lacks the social infectiousness of healthy laughter. Schizophrenic laughter is not appropriate to the context; the schizophrenic laughs at things the majority of humanity recognizes as sad. The laughter of a victim of pseudobulbar palsy occurs even when nothing has taken place which the rest of us commonly accept as being funny.

It is also within the context of this network of human relationships that the distinction between *laughing with* and *laughing at* acquires its meaning, and becomes so important. In cruel laughter, in laughing at someone, we exclude him from the network of love, understanding and support; in laughing with someone, we enfold him within it.

Similar considerations apply when one is trying to

distinguish therapeutic uses of mirth from potentially harmful ones. In order to be therapeutic, it is a pre-condition that the humor be of a type which includes the patient within such warm and comprehensive relationships with fellow human beings.

Even beyond that, however, humor and laughter appear to have specific properties or effects which, under favorable conditions, can be therapeutic, and which may help to explain the instances of apparent healing by humor which have been noted. Kant and Walsh both mention an alleged direct mechanical effect of laughter which they believe to be physiologically beneficial in itself. This kind of principle may be at least partially applicable in some cases—for instance, the mechanical effect of the laughter William Battie produced in his patient helped to burst the abscess—but in most instances it is vastly overemphasized. Other factors must certainly be brought in when one is trying to account for most of the therapeutic uses of mirth described in Chapter II.

Much earlier, it was proposed that one meaning of "having a good sense of humor" was being able to acquire a cosmic perspective on one's problems. This seems to me to have been an important factor in the case of my patient whose severe depression seemed to improve after he was able to laugh at a stressful incident which took place in the cookie factory where he worked. I believe that a real breakthrough for him came during that particular therapeutic session because, at that time, he could view his actions, attitudes and behavior from a somewhat detached and comic perspective, and could use this insight to gain the determination to make the needed changes in his life.

How are we to explain the unusual instances in which

clowns appear to have brought people out of withdrawn states? Perhaps at least the beginning of an explanation lies in considering a factor which humor and withdrawn states share: regression. People who are withdrawn have, in one respect, returned to the helpless state of the infant: They are unable to take care of their basic needs, including taking the initiative in establishing communication with others. We have seen that, from the psychological point of view, there are reasons for characterizing humor as a kind of joint, playful regression. Clowns seem to have a special license to engage in regressive behavior; professional clowns themselves frequently comment on the exhilarating feeling of freedom from customary social restraints which they experience while made up and costumed.

It is not inconceivable that if a person is withdrawn, it may help to regress back to his level to retrieve him. To express this point in the simple form of a spatial metaphor, it is as though the clown were saying to the withdrawn person: "If you cannot or will not come out of your shell, then I will go into it with you and lead you back out."

Humor and laughter may have a more multifaceted role in pain control. Response to pain has been found to have very significant social-cultural determinants, as do humor and the response to it. The importance of one's general outlook—including that of persons with a laughing attitude to life—in pain sensitivity and tolerance is still a relatively neglected, but fertile, area of research.

Also, it is possible that in certain cases the anesthetic effect of mirth resides in a different psychological mechanism. Some aches and pains can be made worse by the very act of paying attention to them. Laughter can take one away from oneself, one's worries. For at least a moment, a person who laughs can forget his troubles. Perhaps humor sometimes works just by withdrawing attention from pain.

Certain kinds of pain are caused, or made worse, by muscle tension which the person is producing himself, although he may not be consciously aware that he is doing so. For example, if a person becomes aware of a minor pain in a small area of his body, and begins to concentrate on it, he may unconsciously tighten up the muscles around that spot. As a consequence, the pain will worsen as the taut muscles themselves begin to ache. Another example of a pain syndrome which is self-generated is the muscle tension headache. Someone becomes anxious or depressed and, without realizing it, begins to tighten the muscles at the back of his head and neck; soon he has a headache.

It is interesting to speculate, therefore, about whether some of the alleged anesthetic benefits of laughter could be related to the decrease in muscle tone which is one of the demonstrable physiological effects of laughter. In that case, the sequence of events would be this: Unconsciously produced tension in the muscles increases, or causes, a headache. The person is presented with a humorous stimulus. He laughs, the tension of his muscles in the affected area decreases, and the pain is relieved.

Another basis for the therapeutic effect of humor may lie in its efficacy in establishing or restoring communication between the doctor and his patient. In medicine, maintaining communications is necessary not only as a social amenity but also because of the importance of securing the patient's cooperation and understanding in both diagnosing and treating his condition. This is highly desirable in any illness, but in some it is absolutely essential. To take only one example: Diabetics often must significantly alter their entire life style in order to live successfully with the disorder. They must learn which foods to eat and which to avoid. They must be shown how to test their urine for sugar, how to regulate their dosage of insulin and how to give themselves injections. None of these or the many other things they must learn can be understood unless there is good doctor-patient communication.

As a good social lubricant, humor may well aid in getting communication established. As I began to practice medicine, one way I naturally began to use humor to advantage was to poke fun at the strange instruments doctors use. The gadgetry of modern medicine looks awesome and frightening to people who are not familiar with it (and sometimes even more awesome and frightening to doctors who *are* familiar with it). Patients who are uneasy and apprehensive when they are about to be probed with an infernal-looking machine can often be put more at ease if the doctor will make a joke about the apparatus.

Children who are being given anesthetic gases through a mask are often terrorized; they are afraid that someone is trying to smother them. Some anesthesiologists solve this problem by making the ugly mask into a funny, friendly hand puppet. The puppet amuses the child for a while by "talking" to him. Finally, he leans over to "kiss" the child, who goes peacefully to sleep.

One final therapeutic effect of humor is conceivably the most important of them all. The will to live is a force which is very hard to define, or to specify precisely; nonetheless, it must be reckoned with in medicine. It sometimes happens that a patient will come into the hospital for a minor ailment or surgical procedure and assert that he is going to die, that he will never get out of the hospital alive. Despite thorough physical examination and laboratory measurements which indicate that the patient is healthy, he does die during his hospital stay. Many physicians have learned to take such remarks by patients very seriously.

The opposite phenomenon takes place, too. Sometimes a patient comes into the hospital and is given a grim prognosis by his physicians. He is told that he has only a few weeks or months of life remaining to him, that it is inconceivable that he will be able to live much longer in his condition. The patient believes otherwise. He asserts that he is not going to die, that he will overcome the condition, and, contrary to prediction, he does live. Some such patients have outlived by decades the doctors who delivered the pronouncements.

All this is an expression, I feel, of factors which we do not as yet understand. At most, of course, the will to live is something which only holds the balance of power in a certain range of cases. Obviously, it cannot make anyone immortal. Nonetheless, despite its ambiguous and at present rather mysterious nature, it may be that there are some cases in which moblizing the patient's will to live is one of the most important things a physician can do.

There is a link between the will to live and the sense of humor. Sigmund Freud put this very well:

> Like wit and the comic, humour has in it a *liberating* element. But it has also something fine and elevating, which is lacking in the other two ways of deriving pleasure from intellectual activity. Obviously, what is fine about it is the triumph of narcissism, the ego's

victorious assertion of its own invulnerability. It refuses to be hurt by the arrows of reality or to be compelled to suffer. It insists that it is impervious to wounds dealt by the outside world, in fact, that these are merely occasions for affording it pleasure. This last trait is a fundamental characteristic of humour.[1]

Perhaps ultimately, and in the deepest sense, humor works by rallying, and by being a manifestation of, the will to live. One of the most hopeful responses I have received on this subject came from a professional comedian who attended one of my presentations on the medical aspects of mirth. Afterwards, he came up and told me that before, on those occasions on which he had really made his audience laugh, he had always told his wife, "I killed them tonight!" Now, he said, he is going to tell her, "I helped them live!"

IX

Humor and the Healing Professions: Restoring the Balance in Modern Medicine

In various ways, society is telling us that the medical establishment itself is sick. There is much discontent about modern medicine, and there are no doubt many different reasons for it. Many of these reasons have been widely aired during the ongoing public debate about health care. Among those which have not, one especially bears upon the theme of this book. It is, in short, that professions tend to take themselves too seriously.

This tendency is regrettable but understandable. On the individual level, one must remember that the training involved in becoming a medical specialist is no small matter. It represents an investment of literally years of labor consisting of untold hours of reading, lectures, and supervised practice. No wonder that, at the end of this ordeal, a doctor is occasionally tempted to marvel at how much he or she knows and to be impressed with the great importance of it all. From the broader perspective, at times some even give the annoying impression that the medical profession believes the public exists for it, rather than the other way around. This self-complacency is more a function of the way the profession is organized as an institution within society, rather than a matter of individual malice.

Bergson even had a name for the expert's tendency toward over-seriousness; he labeled it "professional solemnity." But more to the point than what to call it is this question: Are there any remedies for it?

One might recommend cultivating the habit of occasional awe-inspired recognition of the relative preponderance of our ignorance over our knowledge. This, however, seems to be an exceedingly rare talent among human beings.

Alternatively, one might try to learn from the analyses of what a profession is, as defined by certain sociologists. A profession, they reason, is a subunit within the social order. It exists by virtue of a license from society, which grants to that group a degree of liberty in interpreting, propagating, and using certain specialized knowledge. In exchange, society expects that this knowledge be employed for the public good. The difficulty arises, this analysis suggests, when the profession tries to appropriate for itself the power to make certain moral choices about how this service is to be delivered, a matter which in fact lies beyond the expertise of the profession.

Sadly, this sociological consideration is probably too abstract to be of much immediate benefit, and it is itself likely to be understandable only to professional sociologists.

Perhaps some correctives for professional solemnity can be found in humor. It must not be overlooked that humor already plays an important role in helping doctors deal with the stress which accompanies their own position among the complexities, perplexities and pressures of modern medical practice. Most physicians have their own repertoire of funny stories about the zany complaints they have heard in the early morning hours of the emergency room. What better way is there to cope with the absurdity of being roused from bed at 3 a.m. to treat a patient's sniffles (he has had them, he tells you, for three weeks now!) than to laugh at the incident?

An unexplored avenue of approach lies in attempting to decipher the general public's perception of the medical profession as reflected in popular humor about doctors. It is very interesting that the profession of medicine is one of the most frequent subjects both of informally circulated jokes and of cartoons appearing in the press. Maybe we should pay closer attention to what these jests are telling us about how physicians appear to others.

Conceivably, the best remedy of all for professional solemnity could consist of incorporating humor more self-consciously into the medical curriculum. However, if doctors are ever to be taught to pay more attention to humor and laughter, both as diagnostic and as therapeutic aids, a multitude of issues needs further to be elaborated, explored, and clarified.

For instance, in light of the many contraindications to the use of humor therapy, it is quite obvious that we need to develop a practical way of assessing individual response to humor. We need to find out what kinds of questions can most conveniently, quickly and reliably elicit from a patient the state of his sense of humor; in short, we need to know the best way of taking a humor history.

I have used a set of questions which is brief yet indicative, and at the same time allows for the fact that the response of humor is highly variable among different individuals. One set of questions, for instance, might be: *What sort of role did humor play in the person's family as he was growing up? Was he teased excessively as a child? What kinds of jokes, humor, etc., does he like best? What is the most, or loudest, or longest he has ever laughed on a single occasion? What is his favorite joke? How often does he laugh?* Asking one or more of these questions, or others like them, can yield a good understanding of the patient's response to humor, even during a brief clinical encounter.

Another issue which bears importantly on the feasibility of humor therapy is raised by the fact that, just as there are many types of drugs, so are there many forms of humor. It could turn out that a specific form of humor which is of benefit for some patients under certain conditions, would be detrimental to other patients under different conditions. In one experiment by a group of behavioral scientists, it was determined that laughter responses of audiences of experimental subjects varied in measurable and predictable ways, depending upon the particular comedian to whom they listened.[1] Thus, recordings by one comedian (Phyllis Diller) tended consistently to produce laughs which began very soon after the punch line and came quickly to a peak of volume. Another comedian (Bill Cosby) consistently provoked, in those same audiences, laughter which had its onset after an appreciable delay following the punch line and which reached its peak volume later, subsiding more gradually. Such results suggest the interesting possibility that someday we might find that one kind of comedian is better for a given patient than another would be.

119

One could predict even now, however, that an ultimately more valuable kind of humor therapy would consist not just in telling a patient jokes and getting him to laugh at them, but in helping him to be able to take a humorous perspective on life. If having the type of sense of humor in which one is able to take a comic view of life's ups and downs is important for health, then how does one encourage it in patients? The greatest difficulty here stems from the fact that this type of sense of humor seems either to be a spontaneous, creative phenomenon, or to stem from little understood factors of early development which often lie beyond one's control later in life. If helping the patient achieve a broader perspective on life is one of the therapeutic benefits to be derived from humor, then we must realize that we can hardly help the patient do this until we achieve it in ourselves.

I am not proposing that doctors become comedians. Nor am I recommending that laughter replace the medical techniques that we already have. I propose only that it could be used to supplement them. We are currently spending huge sums of money every year to develop increasingly more sophisticated and sometimes, alas, more toxic chemical agents to combat disease. It is necessary and right that we do so. The amount of money we would have to invest to test one of the most ancient and widespread health beliefs of mankind—namely, that mirth is therapeutic—would be very small in comparison. If any studies along this line were to yield positive results, we would thereby gain an added benefit. For, unlike a pill, or a potion, or an injection, humor itself is one of the good things of life. So, to dispense laughter to someone would be directly to increase the quality of his life.

Finally, I would like to comment on how, sometimes,

seeing oneself, one's profession, and one's technical knowledge in a humorous light can aid immeasurably in understanding the patient's experience and perception of it all. An incident took place some time ago which taught me a lot about medicine, about people, and about how to communicate.

Once, when I was working in a clinic, I received a visit from a young man who, though obviously bright, had only a minimal amount of formal education. He had a tormented grimace on his face as he told me about his problem. There was, he said, an awful, intense, burning pain in his foot, which had begun several days before, and which had even prevented him from sleeping since that time. He had found that if the foot was touched, even lightly, in certain spots, the pain suddenly worsened, reaching almost intolerable levels. So, he had quickly learned effectively to immobilize his foot and to guard it by folding it inward so that no one would inadvertently brush against it and touch one of the trigger zones.

He went on to relate that two weeks before, during a gun battle, he had been shot in the thigh on that side, and that the bullet had gone all the way through. He had received medical attention for this injury and was given a supply of analgesics and antibiotics. It was only after the leg wound was quite well healed, and he had stopped taking the pain-killing medication, that he had noticed the pain in his foot. It was so bad now, he said, that he just couldn't bear it any more.

This man's story and his complex of symptoms constitute a classical presentation of a still incompletely understood disorder called causalgia. It sometimes occurs after a person receives an injury to a nerve in a limb. Sometime afterward, in an area corresponding to the skin distribution of the nerve, the pain begins, and it appears to be associated with a malfunction of the sympathetic nerve fibers which are found in the larger nerve. If causalgia is diagnosed soon enough after its onset, an operation called lumbar sympathectomy, in which the sympathetic nerve chains are interrupted at a point in the back where they enter the spinal cord, often provides dramatic relief of the pain.

So, the surgical residents, were called in, and soon the little examining room was full of impressive figures attired in white coats. Phrases like "causalgia," "peripheral nerve," "sympathetic nervous system," and "lumbar sympathectomy" were being tossed around, with a great air of excitement, in this poor man's presence. Meanwhile, he could only keep begging of us, "Please get this pain stopped. I don't care how you do it. If you have to cut my foot off, go ahead. I don't care!"

After a short while, he was admitted to the hospital and worked up for surgery. He was given papers of consent to sign, and within a short period of time a lumbar sympathectomy had been performed on him.

The surgery went well and the next morning when I went in to see him, he greeted me with a beaming, happy, smiling face. The pain, he said, was completely gone. He could move his foot now with complete ease.

As I was examining him, I suddenly took a humorous perspective on the whole situation as I thought how unfathomable the mysteries of medicine must seem, sometimes, to outsiders. I said to him, "I guess it strikes you as really, really funny that you got shot in your thigh, a few days later you get an awful pain in your foot, then we take you into the hospital to operate on your back and the pain goes away."

He laughed and said, "Yeah, doctor, that sure is amazing. You know, when you put me under the anesthesia I thought you were going to cut my foot off!"

So, in becoming aware of how my own profession must appear in the mind of an uninitiated person, I learned an important lesson in communicating with patients about the apparently bizarre happenings of modern medical treatment. By now, we have all read about those uncanny tales of people who claim, some in all good faith, that they were abducted by the uniformed crews of flying saucers, and physically examined with other-worldly gadgets. I have no notion as to whether or not any of these accounts are true in the classical sense. Frankly, I haven't looked into the details of these stories or their investigation sufficiently to form an intelligent judgment. Setting aside the question of their actual physical reality, however, they are fascinating as caricatures of what the encounter of even a very well-educated layman with the medical establishment must be like these days.

Picture the feelings and thoughts which must go through a patient's mind as he is ushered into an examination cubicle and surrounded by uniformed personnel speaking an indecipherable vocabulary. A paper is shoved under his nose for him to sign as they probe him with instruments he cannot understand. All these happenings must seem terribly bizarre, not all that much less bizarre than being kidnapped and examined by UFO pilots. Perhaps, then, it isn't too far out to approach those reports by asking not only whether they count as evidence of interplanetary visitations, but also whether they might represent mental projections of people's response to the experience of contemporary medical treatment.

In this rather eerie vein, I would like to close with a whimsical thought. For some years now we have been reading that astronomers are debating the value of trying to establish communications with any intelligent life forms which might inhabit planets circling distant stars. Some scientists reason that since we have ourselves now reached a level of technological development at which we have the capacity to detect emanations from remote space, there may well be, somewhere out there, intelligent beings with the same capabilities. If so, there is some chance of overhearing messages they might have beamed in our direction, or, alternatively, of our getting their attention, announcing our presence in the universe by sending them our greetings.

Any two-way communication would depend upon there being some common language between us. Naturally, in our technological age, numerical relationships and concepts were the first terms to be considered as a possible basis for a universal language, and attention was soon focused on the ubiquitous mathematical constant pi—3.1415. . . . It was proposed that we might listen for pi, or perhaps transmit it, to signal that we, too, belong to the brotherhood of sentient life.

However, there are many other forms of communication, even among human beings, than mathematics. As we have seen, one of them is humor. Wouldn't it be funny if the first message that comes to us across those vast, cold interstellar spaces were to be, not pi, but a joke?

Once, when I ended a lecture on that note, a man came up afterward and told me that one could take that thought one step further. He said, "What if we sent out, 'pi-r-square' and they replied, 'No, pie are round!'"

124

Notes

I: A DOCTOR LOOKS AT LAUGHTER

1. Dr. G. V. N. Dearborn, "The Nature of the Smile and Laugh," *Science,* 11, 283, June 1, 1900, 853-854.
2. Quoted in J. C. Gregory, *The Nature of Laughter* (New York: Harcourt, Brace & Co., Inc., 1924), 25.
3. H. A. Paskind, "Effect of Laughter on Muscle Tone," *Archives of Neurology and Psychiatry,* 28, 1932, 623-628.
4. Herbert Spenser, "The Physiology of Laughter," first published in *Macmillan's Magazine,* March, 1860
5. Sigmund Freud, *Jokes and Their Relation to the Unconscious,* James Strachey, trans. (New York: W. W. Norton & Co., Inc., 1960).
6. Stanley Schachter and Ladd Wheeler, "Epinephrine, Chlorpromazine, and Amusement," *Journal of Abnormal and Social Psychology,* 65, 2, 1962, 121-128.
7. James Orchard Halliwell, *Tarlton's Jests and News Out of Purgatory* (London: The Shakespeare Society, 1844), 13.
8. George Meredith, "An Essay on Comedy" in *Comedy* (Garden City, N.Y.: Doubleday Anchor Books, 1956), 42.

II: HEALING BY HUMOR: SOME EXAMPLES

1. Reprinted in *The Saturday Review,* May 28, 1977, 4.
2. Charles Dickens, ed., *Memoirs of Joseph Grimaldi,* Revised version edited by Richard Findlater (London: MacGibbon & Kee Ltd., 1968), 175-177.
3. Mark Zborowski, *People in Pain* (San Francisco: Jossey-Bass, Inc., 1969).

III: HUMOR AND HEALTH: THE HISTORY OF AN IDEA

1. Quoted in James J. Walsh, *Laughter and Health* (New York: D. Appleton and Co., 1928), 147-148.
2. *Ibid.,* 148.
3. *Ibid.*
4. Robert Armin, *A Nest of Ninnies* (London: The Shakespeare Society, 1842), 41.

5. Dr. Doran, *The History of Court Fools* (London: Richard Bentley, 1858), 229.

6. *Nuova Antologia di Scienze, Lettere ed arti.* Terza Serie. Vols. 34, 35. (Rome, 1891).

7. Richard Mulcaster, *Positions* (London: Henry Barnard and R. H. Quick, 1887), 64–65.

8. Robert Burton, *The Anatomy of Melancholy* (New York: Vintage Books), 119–124.

9. J. H. Bernard, ed. and trans., *Kant's Critique of Judgment,* Second edition, revised (London: Macmillan and Co., Ltd., 1914), 222–223, 225.

10. Doran, 230–231.

11. James Sully, *An Essay on Laughter* (New York: Longmans, Green, and Co., 1902), 34–36.

12. William McDougall, "A New Theory of Laughter," *Psyche,* 2, 1922, 298–300.

13. Walsh, vii, viii, xi, 127.

14. Alanson Skinner, *Political Organization, Cults, and Ceremonies of the Plains-Ojibway and Plains-Cree Indians* (New York: American Museum of Natural History, 1914), 501.

IV: LAUGHTER AND DISEASE

1. D. C. Gajdusek and V. Zigas, "Kuru," *American Journal of Medicine,* 26, 1959, 442.

2. Reprinted in Louis S. Goodman and Alfred Gilman, *The Pharmacological Basis of Therapeutics,* Fourth edition (Toronto: The Macmillan Co., 1970), 43.

3. J. Rodier, "Manganese Poisoning in Moroccan Miners," *British Journal of Industrial Medicine,* 12, 1955, 21.

4. Macdonald Critchley, "Periodic Hypersomnia and Megaphagia in Adolescent Males," *Brain,* 85, December 1962.

5. George M. Gould and Walter L. Pyle, *Anomalies and Curiosities of Medicine* (Bell Publishing Co., 1956), 524.

6. *Ibid.*

7. G. Stanley Hall and Arthur Allin, "The Psychology of Tickling, Laughing, and the Comic," *The American Journal of Psychology,* 9, 1, October, 1897, 7.

8. Harald Hoffding, *Outlines of Psychology*, trans. by Mary E. Lowndes (London: Macmillan and Co., 1919).
9. James J. Walsh, *Laughter and Health* (New York: D. Appleton and Co., 1928), xi.

V: LAUGHTER AND MADNESS

1. Robert Burton, *The Anatomy of Melancholy* (New York: Vintage Books), 48–49, 51–52.
2. Charles Baudelaire, *The Essence of Laughter*, ed. by Peter Quennell (New York: Meridian Books, 1956), 115.
3. K. L. Kahlbaum, *Catatonia* (Baltimore: Johns Hopkins University Press, 1973).
4. Emil Kraepelin, *Lectures on Clinical Psychiatry*, revised and ed. by Thomas Johnstone (New York: Hafner Publishing Co., 1968), 24.
5. Eugen Bleuler, *Textbook of Psychiatry*, ed. by A. A. Brill (New York: The Macmillan Co., 1924), 409.
6. *Ibid.*, 544.
7. Burton, 401.
8. Franz Alexander, *Psychosomatic Medicine: Its Principles and Applications* (W. W. Norton, 1950), 56–58.
9. G. Stanley Hall and Arthur Allin, "The Psychology of Tickling, Laughing, and the Comic," *The American Journal of Psychology*, 9, 1, October, 1897, 6–7.

VI: THE PATHOLOGY OF LAUGHTER: OCCUPATIONAL AND IATROGENIC CAUSES

1. Robert Burton, *The Anatomy of Melancholy* (New York: Vintage Books), 339, 341, 342.
2. *Ibid.*, 124.
3. George Meredith, "An Essay on Comedy" in *Comedy* (Garden City, N.Y.: Doubleday Anchor Books, 1956), 4.
4. Lord Chesterfield, *Letters* (London: William Teco, 1872), 250.
5. Saint Chrysostom, *On the Priesthood; Ascetic Treatises; Select Homilies and Letters; Homilies on the Statues*, vol. 9 of *A Select Library of the Nicene and Post-Nicene Fathers of the Christian Church*, Philip Schaff, ed. (New York: The Christian Literature Co., 1889), 442.

6. Chrysostom, 447.

7. Dr. Doran, *The History of Court Fools* (London: Richard Bentley, 1858), 162–163.

8. See Ian Stevenson, "Physical Symptoms Occurring with Pleasurable Emotional States," *American Journal of Psychiatry*, 127, 2, August 1970, 93–97; also, Stevenson, "Physical Symptoms During Pleasurable Emotional States," *Psychosomatic Medicine*, 12, 2, March–April, 1950, 98–102.

9. Garrison, *History of Medicine* (W. B. Saunders, 1929), Reprinted 1966, 156.

10. Maurice Sand, *The History of the Harlequinade* (London: Benjamin Blom, Inc., 1915), 212.

11. Doran, 82–83.

VII: SOCIETY AND HEALING HUMOR

1. Cicero, *Oratory and Orators*, trans., and ed. by J. S. Watson (London: Henry G. Bohn, 1862), 290.

2. Elizabeth S. Haldane and G. R. T. Ross, trans., *The Philosophical Works of Descartes*, vol. 1 (New York: Dover Publications, 1955), 413.

3. J. C. Gregory, *The Nature of Laughter* (New York: Harcourt, Brace & Co., Inc., 1924), 16.

4. *Ibid.*, 17.

5. A. M. Rankin and P. J. Philip, "An Epidemic of Laughing in the Bukoba District of Tanganyika," *The Central African Journal of Medicine*, 9, 5, May 1963.

6. J. F. Coates, "Wit and Humor: A Neglected Aid in Crowd and Mob Control," *Crime and Delinquency*, 18, 1972, 184–191.

7. S. G. Brisland et. al., "Laughter in the Basement," *It's a Funny Thing, Humor*, Antony J. Chapman, ed. (New York: Pergamon Press, 1977).

8. John R. Atkins, "A Designed Locale for Laughter to Reinforce Community Bond," *Ibid.*

IX: HUMOR AND THE HEALING PROFESSIONS: RESTORING THE BALANCE IN MODERN MEDICINE

1. Howard R. Pollio et. al., "Humor, Laughter, and Smiling: Some Preliminary Observations of Funny Behaviors," *The Psychology of Humor: Theoretical Perspectives and Empirical Issues* (Academic Press, 1972).